THE AD MAN

PRINCIPLES FIRST. TECHNOLOGY SECOND.
RESULTS NOW!

BY JIM MUDD SR, CLIFTON LAMBRETH, & ROB MUDD

CONTRIBUTORS:
ALAN MULALLY
KEN BLANCHARD
DARRYL STRAWBERRY

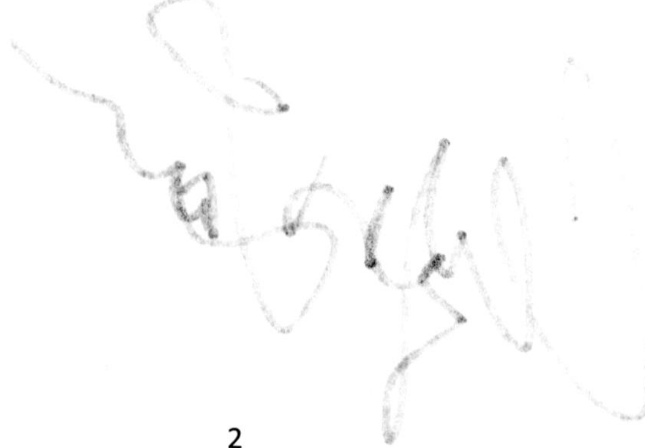

THE AD MAN 2.0

Principles first. Technology second. RESULTS NOW!

Published by MUDD Publishing, a division of MUDD, INC.

915 Technology Parkway

Cedar Falls, IA 50613

319-277-2003

www.Mudd.com

1st edition

ISBN – 978-0-9850139-5-0

Printed in the United States of America

www.mudd.com/TheAdManBook

www.TheAdManBook.com

Contributors

Alan Mulally, Ken Blanchard, Darryl Strawberry

Illustrations, Icons, and Cover Design by Mudd Advertising Artists

Alissa Neubauer, Allie Carty, Dave Hult

Editor

Evan Tovar, Wendy Jermier, Sarah McArthur

Table of Contents

Dedication

By Robert Mudd
Chief Futurist, Mudd Advertising

My father, Jim Mudd Sr., didn't just start an agency—he started a movement. From the basement of our home in 1981, he built a company that stood for something far greater than advertising. It stood for integrity, hustle, community, and above all, people.

Dad believed in hard work and long odds. He built Mudd Advertising the same way a dealer builds trust: one relationship at a time. He didn't have venture capital. He didn't have a tech stack. What he had was vision, resilience, and an unwavering belief in the people he served. That belief became our blueprint.

In 2012, Dad published *The Ad Man*, a book that captured the spirit of the business he built—and the principles that shaped it. The book wasn't just about ads; it was about attitude. About standing for something.

About showing up the next day. And about leading through chaos, not waiting for it to pass.

Today, in an era defined by data, automation, AI, and accelerating change, *The Ad Man 2.0* picks up where he left off. This isn't just an update. It's a reinvention. Because the world has changed—but the truths Dad built this company on haven't.

"If you don't stand for something, you'll fall for anything."
"It isn't the severity, but the proximity, that makes the problem acute."

Those weren't just quotes. They were compass points. And they still guide every decision we make.

In *The Ad Man 2.0*, you'll find more than strategy. You'll find a roadmap for surviving disruption—and turning it into dominance. You'll read about how ZIP codes became audiences, how linear and digital media can dance in perfect sync, and how identity—not just impressions—is the future of automotive retail.

This book isn't just for marketers. It's for dealers, entrepreneurs, family business owners, technologists, and anyone who's ever wondered how to evolve without losing what made you great in the first place.

Dad used to say: "We love it when you succeed." That wasn't a tagline. It was a promise.

And in that spirit, I offer you this next chapter—not just in the Mudd story, but maybe in yours too.

Welcome to *The Ad Man 2.0*.

—Rob Mudd

Acknowledgements

A Reflection of Gratitude

As Jim reached this stage of life, something unexpected began to happen.

Memories didn't return in order. They came quietly, in waves—like a slide show playing on its own. Faces. Voices. Moments of help that once felt ordinary, but with time revealed themselves as guidance at just the right moment.

He began to see how often his path had been steady, sometimes by counsel, sometimes by example, sometimes simply by someone showing up when it mattered most.

There were men of conviction and consistency—John Deery Sr., John Deery Jr., and Dan Deery—who showed him what it meant to build something that could outlive individual success. Ray and Todd Green, whose counsel carried weight because it was earned, were not offered lightly. John McEleney, Mark McKie, Pat Pritchard,

Gene and Charles Gabus—each stepping in at moments when experience mattered more than opinion.

Brooks Hanna became more than a colleague. He became a lifelong friend—thirty-eight years and counting—the kind of relationship formed through shared trials, honest conversations, and mutual respect. Frank McCarthy, through his leadership with NADA, helped shape Jim's understanding of the industry at its highest level. Ira and David Rosenberg, David Hult, and Joel Ginsburg were steady influences—people who challenged him to think bigger while staying grounded in what truly mattered.

And then there were those who arrived later, almost quietly, at precisely the right time,—offering perspective, encouragement, and clarity when the road behind mattered as much as the road ahead.

Clifton Lambreth was one of those people.

Thoughtful. Grounded. A listener first. Clifton had a way of asking the right question—not to impress, but to understand. His encouragement reminded Jim that reflection is not retreat, and that finishing well requires the same faithfulness as starting strong.

Some memories reached back even further.

Herb Yardley, all the way back in the 1980s, in Plantation, Florida—a military man who served in World War II. Jim's father admired his discipline deeply, and so did Jim. Herb taught him that structure isn't restriction; it's freedom when pressure comes, something Jim would come to understand as a quiet gift.

Then there was Bobby Clark—from his father's radio days in 1959—a sixty-five-year friendship built on enthusiasm, presence, and belief in people. Bobby lived a principle Jim never forgot how to find a need and fill it. Visit people in person. Instill confidence. Show up. Over time, Jim realized that was more than good business—it was a way of living.

As Jim sat with the manuscript in front of him, its pages marked and re-marked, another truth settled in.

This story had never been his alone.

Some names surfaced immediately—people whose influence had shaped his thinking long before this book existed. Alan Mulally, whose disciplined optimism and insistence on clarity reinforced Jim's belief that leadership was rooted in truth, teamwork, and shared purpose. Ken Blanchard, whose life's work reflected the idea that learning is a lifelong calling. And Darryl Strawberry, whose journey carried a different kind of wisdom—that redemption, humility, and perseverance often teach lessons no boardroom ever could.

They hadn't simply contributed perspectives. They had reinforced values Jim believed were bigger than any one book.

He also thought about the people who helped make the message visible.

The Mudd Advertising artists—Alissa Neubauer, Allie Carty, and Dave Hult—had translated ideas into images and structure into clarity. They didn't decorate the message; they revealed it. Their work reminded Jim that clarity, when done well, can feel almost generous.

Words, too, required care.

That care came through the steady hands of Evan Tovar, Wendy Jermier, and Sarah McArthur, whose editing sharpened the story without dulling its heart. They asked the questions that protect truth: Does this matter? Is this clear? Is this honest? Jim came to see their work as a form of stewardship.

One name kept returning—not loudly, but faithfully.

Jim Sartorius.

Every complex effort needs someone willing to carry what others don't see. Jim Sartorius had done that from the beginning—organizing, following up, steadying the work when momentum wavered, and protecting its integrity from first draft to final page.

When deadlines tightened or details threatened to unravel, he didn't seek recognition. He brought order. He brought calm. He helped the work finish well.

And finishing well, Jim had learned, was an act of respect—for the people involved, and for the purpose behind the work.

As Jim closed the manuscript for the night, gratitude came more easily than certainty.

This book was never about proving anything.

It was about honoring the people who had shaped a way of thinking—people who believed that principles come first, that technology should serve people, and that results only matter when they are achieved the right way.

No one builds something that lasts alone.

And *The Ad Man 2.0* stood as quiet testimony to that truth.

Believe you can, and you can. Belief is one of the most powerful of all Problem Dissolvers. When you Believe that a Difficulty can be overcome, you are more than halfway to Victory over It Already.
NORMAN VINCENT PEALE

Foreword

By Alan Mulally

When I read *The Ad Man 2.0*, I was reminded of a lesson that has stayed with me throughout my career: the role of leadership is to create clarity, alignment, and a relentless focus on working together toward a shared purpose.

This book is not about advertising tactics. It is about building organizations that perform — consistently — in an increasingly complex world.

In times of change, leaders are often tempted to move faster by adding more tools, more technology, or more rules. But the organizations that succeed over the long term do something different. They slow down long enough to get aligned on principles, to face reality with facts, and to ensure that everyone understands the plan

— and their role in it.

That is the spirit of *The Ad Man 2.0*.

Throughout the book, you will see a familiar pattern:

See clearly. Align systems. Measure honestly. Learn continuously. Work together.

This is not theoretical. It is how high-performing organizations operate.

During my time leading large, complex enterprises, one of the most powerful tools we used was a disciplined Business Plan Review weekly cadence. The purpose of those reviews was not to judge people. It was to create a shared understanding of reality, to ask the right questions, and to solve problems together. When leaders focus on facts rather than fear, transparency replaces defensiveness — and progress accelerates.

You will see this same mindset throughout this book.

Jim Mudd and Clifton Lambreth emphasize that data is not a replacement for leadership — it is a tool that

strengthens it. Systems do not exist to control people; they exist to enable people to make better decisions more consistently. Technology, when aligned with clear principles and sound processes, becomes a powerful accelerator rather than a distraction.

This is also a book about alignment.

In any organization, performance improves when everyone is pulling in the same direction. That requires a shared vision, a comprehensive strategy, common metrics, and a way of working together that encourages significant and comprehensive collaboration. Whether you are running a dealership, a marketing organization, or a global enterprise, the principle is the same: one team, one plan, and one set of facts.

What I appreciate most about *The Ad Man 2.0* is its message of respect for people. The authors understand that results are produced by individuals who want to contribute, who want to learn, and who want to succeed together. Leadership, at its best, creates an environment where people feel safe telling the truth, raising concerns early, and improving every day. This book offers incredible value in a practical framework for thinking clearly, leading responsibly, and building organizations that can adapt without losing their identity.

If you approach this book the way you would a good Business Plan Review — open, curious, and focused on learning — it will serve you well.

Read it carefully. Discuss it with your team. Apply its principles consistently.

And most importantly, remember that success is never about one individual. It is always about "Working Together"™ — aligned, informed, and committed to continuous improvement.

— Alan Mulally

Former President and CEO of Boeing Commercial Airplanes & Former President and CEO of Ford Motor Company

Introduction

By Ken Blanchard

When I sat down and read The Ad Man, it put a smile on my face for two reasons.

First, although it is a fictional story, I knew it was about the amazing journey that Jim Mudd has been on for decades to create, from scratch, one of the premier advertising agencies in the automotive field. It's a story not just about Jim, but about his wife, his kids, clients, and the ups and downs and joys and challenges of creating a great family business and learning culture. The Ad Man is not just about business; it's about life and how learning is truly a never-ending process.

I don't know two leaders who model what I have

taught about more than Jim Mudd and Clifton Lambreth. They both are looking constantly for ways to serve others, and you will see good examples my philosophy throughout *The Ad Man 2.0*.

When Jim or Clifton learns something new, they are eager to share it with others. Their excitement and enthusiasm have helped many on their journey toward continuous improvement.

They are always open to feedback and self-evaluation as well as counsel from others who might mentor them. I don't know two people who open their world or walk toward wisdom more than Jim and Clifton.

I know that *The Ad Man 2.0* will not only be a good read, but it will also help you on your journey to be a great leader. Enjoy and apply what you learn.

Ken Blanchard

Coauthor of The One Minute Manager®

We love it when
you succeed!

Chapter 1

Life Lessons of the Automotive Dealer's Friend

"There are friends, there is family and there are friends that become family."

Forty years is a long time to build something. It's even longer when you realize it may soon need to run without you.

Jim sat alone in his office as the late afternoon light stretched across the floor. The building was quiet now—phones silent, doors closed, the steady rhythm of the day finally slowed. He had always liked this hour. It was when the noise faded, and the truth surfaced.

For more than four decades, he had helped build a business that shaped other companies. Thousands of clients. Countless strategies. Entire organizations changed—not overnight, but deliberately, decision by decision.

Yet what unsettled him wasn't how much they had accomplished. It was how quickly it had happened. The question pressing on him now wasn't *what had worked.* It was *what would last*.

The Promise on the Wall

On the wall across from his desk hung a simple phrase, framed years ago but never treated as decoration: *"We love it when you succeed."*

Those words weren't marketing copy. They were a promise.

They had justified the long nights, the hard conversations, and the willingness to challenge clients—and themselves—when comfort threatened growth. Success, Jim believed, was never accidental. It was earned through focus, discipline, and the courage to take calculated risks while others waited for certainty.

Celebrations followed effort, not entitlement.

Jim remembered when those words first went on the wall. It was 1982, in a basement office with a desk from a garage sale, a phone, and a dream. His wife, Cecelia, had helped him paint it. Their children had drawn the frame. Back then, it wasn't a motto—it was a prayer. *Please let us help people succeed.*

Now, forty years later, that promise had taken on new weight.

Success had come. The company had grown beyond anything he could have imagined in that basement. They'd helped thousands of dealers, each one of them a real person with a family depending on them. Some had doubled their market share. Others had survived downturns that would have crushed them without a clear strategy. A few had passed their businesses to their children with pride instead of fear.

And Jim had been there for every chapter.

But Jim also knew something most leaders eventually discover: *What gets you here won't get you there.*

The Shelf of Yesterday's Ideas

As he leaned back in his chair, his eyes drifted to a shelf lined with binders—old campaign plans, strategic frameworks, and handwritten notes from meetings long past. At the time, each idea had been cutting-edge. Each had delivered results. And each, eventually, had been replaced.

Not because it was wrong. Because the world had changed.

Jim pulled one binder from the shelf at random. It was labeled "*Digital Strategy 2008.*" He opened it. The work was solid—genuine creativity applied to a real problem. Two pages in, he found a note in his own handwriting: *"This will change everything for dealers."*

It had, for a season.

But that season had passed, and Jim hadn't clung to it. He'd evolved. The company had evolved. But the insight that struck him now, holding that 2008 strategy in his hands, was this: *What if the people who come after me don't evolve the way we did?*

Over the years, Jim had learned that success rarely fails loudly. It fades quietly. It slips into meetings where the same ideas resurface. Into teams that stop questioning assumptions. Into leaders who protect what they've built instead of preparing for what comes next.

He had seen it across industries, not just automotive.

A manufacturing firm that had dominated its market for thirty years went bankrupt after refusing to adapt to new materials. A family business, brilliant for two generations, stumbled when the third generation inherited the title but not the hunger. A dealership group that had been a model for others slowly lost relevance because leadership decided they had already learned everything they needed to know.

The most successful leaders—whether running dealerships, manufacturing firms, service companies, or startups—shared a common trait: *they stayed curious longer than others stayed confident.* That curiosity had shaped everything Jim did.

Built on Borrowed Wisdom

The tools his company developed weren't invented in isolation. They were built by studying what worked in the world's best organizations—inside and outside the automotive industry. Jim and his team borrowed proven ideas, tested them relentlessly, and reshaped them to fit each client's reality, always respecting the brand, the culture, and the people who would have to live with the results.

Jim never believed in one-size-fits-all solutions. People didn't work that way. Businesses didn't either.

Years ago, Jim had learned this lesson the hard way. Early in his career, he'd tried to apply the same advertising formula to every dealership. It didn't work. A strategy that worked for a high-volume urban dealer in the North bombed with a rural dealer in the South. A campaign that fired up a new GSM fell flat with an old-school owner who'd built his business on handshake deals and relationships.

That's when Jim had shifted his approach. Instead of being an expert who told dealers what to do, he became a student of dealers—asking questions, listening to their stories, understanding what made each one unique. He studied how they thought, how they made decisions, what kept them up at night.

The irony wasn't lost on him: *the more he learned to listen, the more valuable his advice became.*

That's also when Jim started building relationships with other mentors and teachers— people like John, people who understood that leadership was about more than strategy. It was about seeing people clearly and helping them become their best selves.

Why Automotive Dealers Matter

What drew Jim to automotive dealers in particular was

their grit. Their independence. Their connection to the community. They weren't faceless corporations. They were employers, sponsors, mentors, and neighbors. They built businesses that supported families—both their own and those they served.

Jim remembered one dealer who used to say, "I don't sell cars. I help people get where they need to go." That mindset, Jim knew, was the difference between a transaction and a *legacy.*

He'd watched that dealer hire people who might not have gotten a chance elsewhere. He'd seen him donate to the local high school, sponsor the little league team, and show up at the hospital when one of his customers was struggling. The man didn't post about it on social media. He just did it.

And his business thrived—not because of his advertising strategy, but because people knew him.

They trusted him. They sent their families to him.

That's the kind of legacy we help build, Jim often thought.

But *his legacy* was under pressure now, more than ever.

The World Is Changing Faster

Markets were shifting faster than ever. Technology rewrote expectations overnight. Customers demanded more transparency, more speed, more value. Consolidation reshaped entire industries. The rules kept changing—and leaders who waited for stability often waited too long.

Jim had watched the automotive industry transform three times in his career. Each time, some dealers adapted and thrived. Others couldn't let go of what had worked before, and they eventually closed their doors. Change, Jim had learned, wasn't the enemy. Complacency was.

Mudd Advertising had been built on a simple truth: *consumers never stop changing, and leaders who stop adapting eventually fall behind.* Staying on the leading edge required courage—acting before change became unavoidable, investing before results demanded it, and learning faster than competitors were comfortable doing.

That courage had carried the company for decades. But now, Jim faced a different challenge—one that couldn't be solved by simply adapting faster.

The Succession Question

Succession.

It had always been a distant concept—important, but not urgent. Now it sat squarely in front of him. The thought wasn't upsetting because he feared stepping away. It was unsettling because he cared deeply about what would remain.

What happens to a mission when the founder leaves? What happens to values when leadership changes hands? What happens when the promise on the wall—*"We love it when you succeed"*—gets passed to someone else to keep?

These questions weighed on him as his phone rang,

breaking the silence. It was John—an old friend, a fellow traveler, someone who never called without reason.

A Dealer's Burden

John had been Jim's first real client back in 1981. Over four decades, they'd become more than client and consultant. They'd become brothers in the work—two men committed to building something that lasted.

But the tone in John's voice that afternoon told Jim something had shifted. "I need to talk," John said simply.

They arranged to meet the next morning at John's dealership. Jim had been there hundreds of times over the years, watched it grow from a modest operation to one of the region's most respected auto groups. He'd celebrated the openings of new locations, the hiring of good people, the victories large and small.

But today, as Jim pulled into the parking lot and saw John waiting by the door, he sensed something different.

They sat in John's office—the same office where he had first offered Jim the chance to build an advertising agency all those years ago. As they talked, Jim shared what had been on his mind: the responsibility of transition, the fear of losing what mattered most, the uncertainty of what came next.

John listened quietly, then surprised him. "I'm dealing with the same thing," he said. The admission changed the tone of the conversation.

John explained that his son wanted to come into the business. It should have been good news. It was, and it was also terrifying. John had built something over four decades. Now he had to let it go, knowing that his son would do things differently.

"The boy wants to bring in consultants, change our systems, try new approaches," John said. "Part of me is proud. Part of me wants to tell him, 'No, do it *my way*.'"

Jim understood. He'd watched it happen a hundred times with dealership owners and their successors. The old guard clings to tradition. The next generation pushes for change— tension brews between.

"You don't want to hand someone a business," John added, looking directly at Jim. "You want to hand them a way of thinking." That sentence stayed with Jim long after they left John's office that morning.

Systems could be documented. Processes could be taught. Spreadsheets could be downloaded. But *judgment*—judgment was developed. It came from experience, reflection, and the willingness to learn from both success and failure.

It took time.

It took mentorship.

It took someone who cared enough to challenge you when you were wrong, and believe in you even when you doubted yourself.

What This Book Really Is

Jim realized something in that moment with John.

This book wasn't about advertising.

It was about *leadership*.

It was about what happens when growth outpaces certainty, when markets shift faster than playbooks, when leaders must decide not just *how to win*—but *how to endure*.

It was about the choice every leader faces: *Do I protect what I've built, or do I prepare for what comes next?*

This book is for anyone who has ever felt the weight of responsibility for people, not just performance.

It's for the dealer owner who's spent forty years building an empire and is asking, "What happens when I'm gone?"

It's for the young leader—the GM, the manager, the salesperson—who's asking, "How do I build something meaningful? How do I become someone worth following?"

It's for the business owner in any industry who knows the market is changing and feels the pressure to change faster, but wonders if speed will cost them their soul.

It's for the son or daughter stepping into their parents' business, trying to honor what came before while creating something new.

For all of you: this book is a journey, not a destination.

In the chapters ahead, Jim will share lessons forged through decades of real-world experience—lessons about adapting to change without losing identity, building systems that scale without burning people out, and leading with purpose when the path forward isn't clear.

These are not theories. They are life lessons.

The Road Ahead

That night, Jim left the office later than usual. The parking lot was nearly empty as he locked the door behind him. The road ahead was uncertain, but for the first time in months, it didn't feel heavy.

It felt necessary.

At home, as he prepared for bed, Jim paused to reflect. He thanked God for the mentors who had guided him—Don Hunt, who had introduced him to faith and possibility. Ray Green, who believed in him when he was starting out. The Deery family, who taught him about business. Brooks Hanna and so many others who had challenged him to be better.

He thanked God for the clients who had trusted him, for the friends who had challenged him when growth demanded discomfort, and for Cecelia—his partner in every sense—who had believed in his dream from that basement office to now.

He asked for clarity—not certainty—as he stepped into what came next. He asked for the wisdom to know what to hold onto and what to let go. And he asked for the strength to become the kind of mentor and leader the next generation could learn from, as he had learned from those who came before. This wasn't an ending.

It was an invitation. An invitation to explore what really matters in building a business that lasts. An invitation to understand that leadership isn't about perfection—it's about consistency, curiosity, and courage—an invitation to discover that the greatest leaders aren't the ones who have all the answers.

They're the ones who ask the best questions, listen carefully, and stay humble enough to keep learning.

And with that realization, a new journey began.

The next morning, Jim would return to his office and begin writing. Not a business manual. Not a case study. But a story about what it really takes to build something that endures, told through the lives of the leaders and the lessons that have shaped him.

For anyone ready to listen. *"You can't expect to win if you don't show up every day."*

Ad Man Notes – Key Principles:

Lesson 1: Success That Lasts Is Built on Curiosity, Not Confidence

The most enduring leaders remain curious longer than others remain certain. Confidence can freeze growth; curiosity sustains it.

Lesson 2: Legacy Is a Way of Thinking, Not a Set of Tactics

You don’t pass down answers — you pass down judgment, principles, and decision frameworks that survive changing markets.

Lesson 3: Change Isn’t the Threat — Complacency Is

Markets will always evolve. Leaders fail not because change arrives, but because they wait too long to respond.

YOUR KEY NOTES

LOCATION.
BEHAVIOR.
DECISION.

Chapter 2

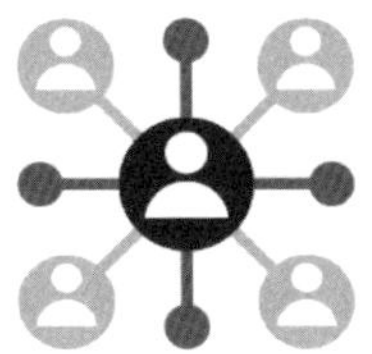

ZIP Code Intelligence: Why Geography Becomes Strategy

"Common Sense must become Common Practice in a world where Common Sense has become less Common."

The Invitation

The invitation arrived the next morning.

Jim's phone rang before 8 AM. The voice on the other end was calm, confident, and deliberate, the kind of voice that didn't waste words. "Hi, Jim. I'm a friend of John's. We're having an important meeting tomorrow at our dealership in Midtown. John thought you should be there."

Jim wrote down the address and time, agreed to attend, and thanked him. When the call ended, Jim paused. He had forgotten to ask what the meeting was about.

He smiled.

Over the years, Jim had learned that John never sent him somewhere without a purpose. These weren't casual introductions or social obligations. They were assignments—carefully chosen moments designed to reveal something Jim needed to see, understand, or think differently about.

Whatever waited at that dealership, John believed it mattered. That was enough for Jim.

He hung up the phone and sat back in his chair. The morning light was just beginning to fill his office. Jim thought about the conversation with John the day before. *"You want to hand them a way of thinking,"* John had said.

This meeting, Jim sensed, was part of that. John was showing him something—not just about advertising or strategy, but about the way of thinking that made great leaders different.

Jim spent the rest of that day in his own thoughts, preparing himself to observe, to listen, and most importantly, to understand the deeper principle behind whatever Bill wanted to teach.

Arriving Before Dawn

Jim arrived early the next morning, parking well before the dealership stirred to life. The air felt still, expectant. The sun hadn't fully cleared the horizon. A few lights glowed in the service bays—technicians already at work, prepping for the day.

This was the mark of a disciplined organization. Work didn't start when customers arrived. It began before the world woke up.

As Jim stepped out of the car, a man approached, hand

extended. He was tall, with silver hair and the kind of bearing that came from decades of running a business. His grip was firm but warm.

"Bill," he said. "John told me you'd be early." They shook hands. Jim noticed Bill's right hand. There it was—the same ring John wore—a capital "S" inscribed on it. The ring appeared on more of John's friends than Jim had realized. He'd have to ask about it eventually.

Bill led Jim inside, past service bays and offices already showing signs of disciplined order. Nothing felt accidental. Technicians were organized by station. Parts were sorted by category. The waiting area had fresh coffee, clean magazines, and comfortable seating. Even at this early hour, the operation hummed with quiet efficiency.

"My family's coming in," Bill said as they climbed the stairs to the conference room. "We're walking through something foundational to our success. I want them to understand the logic—not just the tactics. Not just the 'what,' but the 'why.'"

He paused at the conference room door, turning back to Jim. "Most people use this every day and never realize what it really is. They apply it without understanding it. And when they apply something without understanding it, they eventually abandon it when times get hard or when the world changes."

Jim nodded. He'd seen this pattern countless times—a strategy that worked, but the people implementing it didn't understand why it worked. So when circumstances shifted, they didn't know how to adapt. They just gave up.

"That's why you want them to understand," Jim said.

"Exactly," Bill said.

The Room Is Ready

The conference room itself was a teaching space. Whiteboard on one wall. Flip charts on another. A large screen for projections. Chairs were arranged in a semicircle so everyone could see and be seen.

Bill explained that this setup wasn't accidental either. "When people are seated in rows, they're passive. Rows say, 'Sit back and receive.' When they're in a circle or facing each other, they're active. They think. They contribute. They own the idea."

The family filtered in over the next ten minutes. Bill's two sons, his daughter, a son-in-law, and his two grandchildren—all old enough to understand what was being taught, young enough to potentially lead the business into the future.

Laptops opened. Notebooks came out. Pens were tested. No one was scrolling phones. No one had their eyes half-closed, waiting for this to be over. There was attention in the room. Jim noticed that.

Bill's family knew they were about to learn something important.

The Question Before the Lesson

Before diving into the content, Bill did something that struck Jim immediately. He asked a question.

"Before we go into this," Bill said, looking around the room, "I want each of you to answer one thing. Why does our dealership succeed? What's the foundation? What's the ONE thing that, if we lost it, everything else would fall apart?"

The family sat with this for a moment. Then the answers started coming.

"The customers?" one son offered.

"The people who work here," the daughter said.

"Our reputation," another son added.

"Good products," the grandson offered.

Bill listened to each answer without judgment. Then he smiled. "Those are all real. Those all matter. But there's something underneath all of those. There's something that creates the foundation that allows customers to come, allows good people to stay, and allows reputation to build."

He paused, allowing anticipation to simmer. "It's not the dealership itself," Bill said. "It's the market we've chosen to serve."

Bill stepped toward the whiteboard.

The Zip Code Nobody Sees

"I want to talk about zip codes," Bill said. A few smiles appeared. This didn't sound revolutionary. At least not yet.

But Bill's tone shifted. His voice took on the quality of someone sharing something sacred. "In 1963, the United States Postal Service faced a crisis," he began. "Mail sorting was slow. Delivery was inconsistent. Routes were inefficient. The system was breaking down under its own weight. So they created zip codes to bring order to chaos."

The first slide appeared on the screen:

NOTHING IN THE UNITED STATES MOVES

WITHOUT A ZIP CODE

"Think about that," Bill said. "Mail. Media. Money. Goods. Data. People. Attention. Everything moves through geography. And zip codes are the infrastructure that makes movement possible."

Jim felt it land.

Bill continued, "Zip codes didn't create geography. They revealed it. They made invisible patterns visible. And when you can see patterns, you can understand behavior."

Bill turned back to the family. "Most of you know I spent thirty years in the postal and logistics industry before coming into automotive," he said. "Zip codes saved that system. They transformed it from chaos into order. And years later, when I started in car sales, I realized zip codes could transform that system too."

He advanced the slide:

AUDIENCE BUILDING = BUYING MARKETS, NOT

MEDIA

"Here's where most companies get it wrong," Bill said. "They think marketing is about channels. Digital versus traditional. TV versus social. Radio versus email. That becomes the argument—which channel is best?"

He shook his head. "That's the wrong question entirely. Marketing isn't about channels. Marketing is about where people live—because behavior clusters geographically."

Bill pulled up a map of the city. Zip codes were outlined in different colors. "Each one of these zip codes has its own personality," he explained. "Different income levels. Different household types. Different life stages. Different purchase behaviors. Different media consumption habits. Different vehicle preferences. Different brand loyalties."

He zoomed in on one zip code. "Let's say this is a high-income suburban area. Families. Multiple cars per household. New vehicle purchases every three to five years. They read the newspaper. They watch cable news. They listen to NPR. They shop at specific retailers."

He switched to another zip code. "Now, this is urban, younger, lower income. Single occupancy. Older vehicles. Less frequent new purchases. Digital native. Social media is their newspaper. They stream rather than subscribe to cable."

Bill looked back at the family, commanding their gaze. "Same city. Different zip codes. *Different everything*."

He stood back from the map. "You don't market to a city," he continued. "You market to neighborhoods. You market to a zip code. Because when you understand the zip code, you understand the people. And when you understand the people, you understand what they need."

And like that, he moved on.

From Geography to Behavior

The following slides layered insight on insight, each building on the last.

Zip codes enabled **cross-channel unification**—direct mail reinforcing digital, digital amplifying broadcast,

broadcast validating brand presence. Nothing worked in isolation. Everything worked in sequence, like notes in a symphony rather than sounds in chaos.

"Zip codes are the DNA of marketing," Bill said. "They're the common language that connects platforms that don't naturally talk to each other. Digital marketing people speak one language. Traditional media people speak another. Direct mail has its own vocabulary. But zip codes? Zip codes speak the language of *behavior*. That's the universal translator."

Bill introduced the concept of **Now Market**—shoppers who weren't just browsing or dreaming about a car purchase, but were actually in the window of decision-making. By analyzing transaction data, search behavior, credit inquiries, and other behavioral indicators within ZIP Codes, his team could identify where urgency lived before competitors even noticed demand was building.

"At any given time," Bill explained, "about 15 percent of the market is in a buying window. They're ready. They're comparing. They're close to a decision. The other 85 percent? They're not. Some are years away from a purchase. Some won't buy for a decade."

He let this sink in.

"The massive mistake," Bill continued, "is treating all 100 percent the same way. You send the same message, the same offer, the same urgency to people who are years away from a purchase and people who are weeks away. That's marketing malpractice."

He pointed to the screen. "Zip codes tell you who's in the 15 percent. More importantly, they tell you who's about to enter the 15 percent. And that is where advantage lives."

Bill showed how zip-level insights influenced everything downstream:

- Inventory mix – Which vehicles to stock in which locations
- Messaging tone – Urgent versus educational versus lifestyle-focused

- Creative timing – Which zip codes to hit which odes with which messages
- Offer structure – Which incentives resonated where
- Media weighting – Where to spend the advertising budget for maximum return

"Zip codes don't just tell us who to talk to," Bill said. "They tell us what to say and when to say it."

Jim glanced at the family. They weren't taking casual notes anymore. They were thinking. One of the sons had his pen paused above his notebook, eyes distant. The grandson was leaning forward. The daughter was nodding slightly—recognition that something important was connecting in her mind.

The Cost of Not Seeing

Then Bill did something no statistic could accomplish—he told a story.

"Five years ago," Bill said, "I made a decision that cost

us about $2 million in opportunity. I wanted to advertise a new vehicle—a truck—across the entire city. I created one campaign. One message. One offer. I splashed it everywhere."

He shook his head, remembering. "The truck sold okay. Nothing special. I was disappointed. I thought the vehicle wasn't right, or the market was saturated, or the timing was off."

Bill paused. "Two years later, a consultant came in and did a zip code analysis of where those trucks actually sold. You know what he found?"

Silence.

He swallowed his pride and explained. "Seventy percent of the sales came from four specific zip codes. Not scattered across the city. Concentrated. In four neighborhoods, that truck was perfect. In other areas? Nobody wanted it."

Bill leaned against the front of the room. "I'd spent the same amount of money marketing that truck everywhere.

If I had understood zip codes then, I would have spent 80 percent of my budget on those four zip codes and gotten, conservatively, three times the result. That's $2 million I threw away by not seeing what was invisible without data."

The family absorbed this. It wasn't abstract anymore. It was money. It was a waste. It was the difference between good leadership and outstanding leadership.

"Zip codes force you to see," Bill said. "They remove the option of guessing."

Jim Steps In as Guide

Bill turned to Jim with something unspoken in his eyes. "John told me you'd see the bigger picture," Bill said.

Jim stood, moving toward the whiteboard. This was the moment. The transition from technique to principle. From tactic to philosophy.

Jim picked up the marker; it was *his* turn. "What you've built here," Jim said, "isn't a targeting tactic. It's a leadership lens. It's a way of thinking."

He drew three words in a vertical line on the whiteboard:

LOCATION

BEHAVIOR

DECISION

He stepped back, letting the framework sit.

"Most organizations start at the bottom," Jim said. "They make decisions first. They decide which offer to run, what message to send, and which channel to use. Then they look for data to justify those decisions. They're married to the decision before they even understand the market."

Jim tapped the board at the bottom word. "Great leaders reverse the order."

He tapped LOCATION.

"You start here. You ask, 'Where do people live? What's the geography of opportunity?' You don't judge it. You don't wish it were different. You see it clearly."

His marker moved up. "From there, you understand how people in those locations behave. Not how you want them to behave. Not how they used to behave. How they actually behave, right now, based on data and evidence."

He moved to DECISION.

"Only then—*only then*—do you make a decision. And because you've done the work of seeing and understanding, the decision is almost inevitable. It's not guesswork. It's clarity."

Jim turned to the group. "This applies to any industry. Healthcare. Education. Retail. Financial services. Manufacturing. Nonprofits. Startups. Zip codes tell you where trust exists, where urgency exists, where opportunity exists, and where you're wasting energy trying to convince someone who isn't ready to be convinced."

Jim looked directly at Bill's family. "This is how great leaders think. They see reality clearly. They don't argue with reality. They work with it."

He paused, letting his message resonate, then continued, "This is also how great leaders prepare for the future. Because the people who come after you—your successors, the next generation—they need to learn to think this way. Not just apply zip codes. Do not just use a tool. But understand the principle: *See clearly. Understand behavior. Then decide.*"

Jim put the marker down. "That's what you're teaching today. Not a tactic. *A way of thinking*."

Bill nodded slowly. The family was utterly speechless, present in a way that suggested learning was actually happening.

The Deeper Conversation

Later, alone in Bill's office, he explained to Jim how ZIP-based strategies had reshaped not only his marketing approach, but his leadership as a whole.

"Before zip codes, I was reactive," Bill said. "I'd run a

promotion and hope it worked. I'd see results and try to reverse-engineer why they happened. I was always behind."

He leaned back in his chair. "Zip codes made me proactive. They gave me discipline. I could look at the market and say, 'Here's what's happening. Here's where opportunity is. Here's where I'm wasting money.' It wasn't hope. It was sight."

Jim understood immediately. Discipline wasn't restriction—it was freedom. Freedom to say no to opportunities that didn't fit the market. Freedom to focus resources where they would actually work. Freedom to act decisively instead of tentatively.

"The other thing zip codes taught me," Bill continued, "was humility. I had to admit that my gut—my intuition, which I'd trusted for years—wasn't as reliable as I thought. The data showed me things I'd been wrong about. And when I surrendered to the data instead of defending my intuition, everything got better."

Bill paused, then said, "That's the leadership lesson, really. Humility. Willingness to see what's true instead of what we want to be true."

The Drive Home

Driving home that afternoon, Jim reflected on what he'd witnessed.

Zip codes weren't magic.

They were grounded.

In a world flooded with dashboards, metrics, and noise—so much noise that leaders could rationalize almost any decision if they listened to the right podcast, read the right article, or talked to the right consultant—ZIP Codes anchored strategy to geographic reality.

They forced leaders to confront what is, rather than what we prefer. That was the real advantage.

But something else struck Jim as he drove. This wasn't just about advertising. This was about succession.

Bill had spent his entire meeting teaching his family—the people who would one day run this business—a way of thinking, not just a set of tactics. He was teaching them that outstanding leadership meant seeing clearly before acting, not being brilliant, not being ambitious, not being well-intentioned.

Being clear.

Being grounded in reality.

Jim thought back to his conversation with John. *"You want to hand them a way of thinking."*

Bill was doing precisely that. He was showing his family that when you understand people—really understand them, geographically, behaviorally, emotionally—everything else becomes easier. Decisions come faster. Confidence grows. You stop second-guessing yourself.

And when the world changes, when markets shift, when new technology emerges—you have a framework for thinking about it. You don't have to start over. You just apply the same principle in a new context.

That's what made great leaders prepare the next generation well.

The Framework Crystallizes

That night, Jim would later recognize this day as the moment the first pillar of his leadership framework crystallized:

See the Market Clearly Before You Act

This wasn't about data for data's sake. It wasn't about analytics as an end in themselves. It was about alignment—between strategy and reality, between message and market, between leadership intent and customer need.

Zip code intelligence was the starting point, but the principle went deeper. Seeing clearly meant:

- Understanding your customer before designing your offer

- Recognizing geographic, demographic, and behavioral patterns
- Admitting what's true about your market instead of what you wish were true
- Using data to inform intuition, not replace it
- Building strategy on a foundation of reality, not hope

And once a leader learned to see clearly, everything that followed— messaging, timing, resource allocation, hiring, systems, training—became more effective because it was aligned with what was actually true about the market and the people they served.

Jim understood now why John had sent him here.

This wasn't just about zip codes.

It was about the most fundamental leadership skill: the ability to see what's actually true.

The Central Takeaway

That night, Jim wrote one sentence in his notebook:

When leaders learn to see geography as behavior—and behavior as a window into human need—marketing becomes strategy, and strategy becomes leadership.

Zip codes weren't the story.

They were proof.

And Jim knew that once leaders truly understood this principle—that clear sight leads to confident action—they would never see their markets, their teams, or their future the same way again.

Because they would have learned to see.

And seeing, truly seeing, was where all outstanding leadership began.

"The truth works."

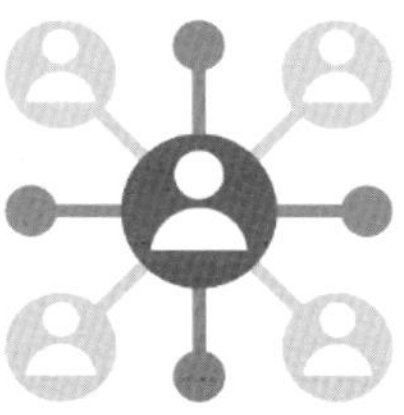

Ad Man Notes – Key Principles:

Lesson 1: You Don't Market to Cities — You Market to Behavior

Geography reveals behavior. ZIP Codes make invisible demand patterns visible and actionable.

Lesson 2: Clarity Comes Before Creativity

When leaders see the market clearly, decisions become obvious. Guesswork disappears when reality is visible.

Lesson 3: The Best Leaders Reverse the Decision Order

Start with location → understand behavior → then decide. Leaders who decide first and justify later waste time and money.

YOUR KEY NOTES

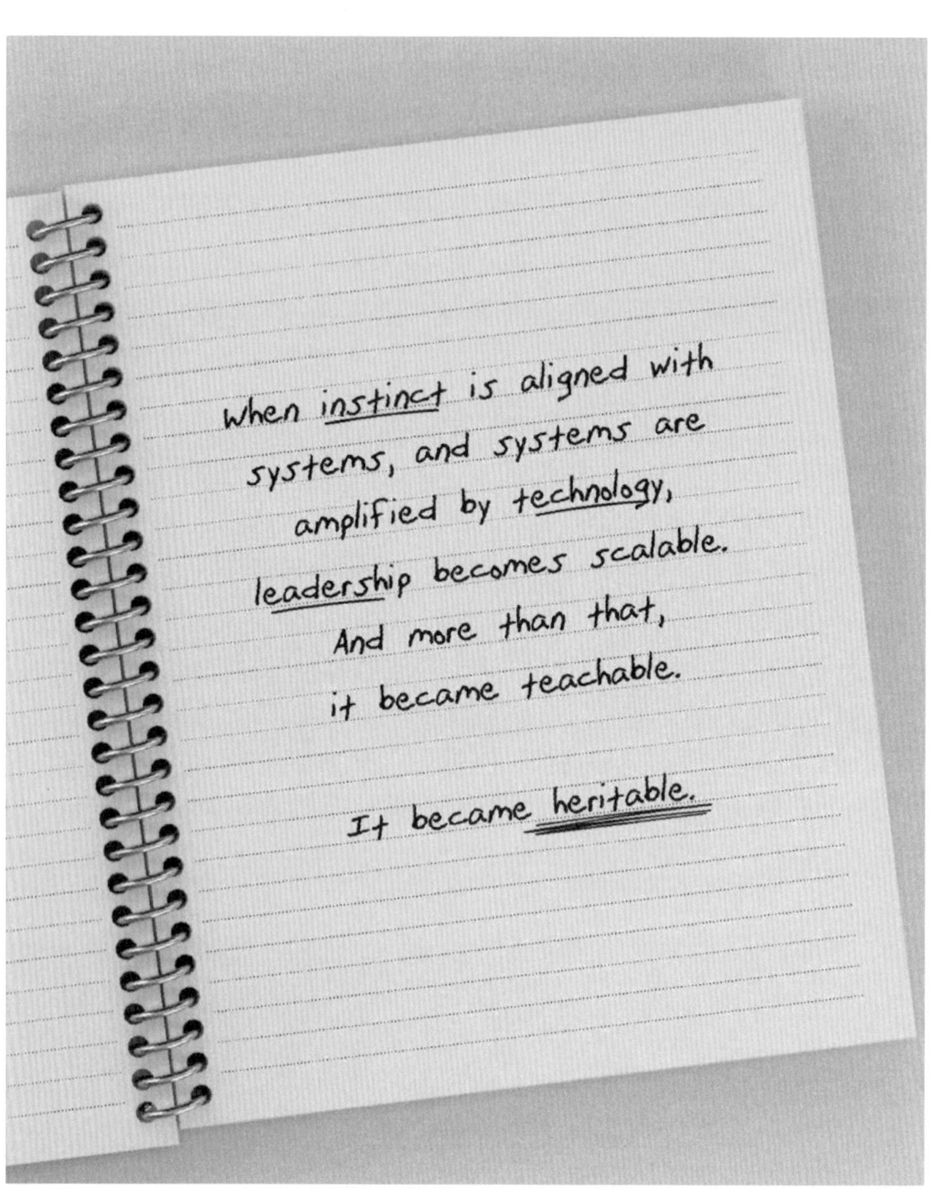
When instinct is aligned with
systems, and systems are
amplified by technology,
leadership becomes scalable.
And more than that,
it became teachable.
It became heritable.

Chapter 3

Aligning Systems to Behavior

"Behavior is always greater than knowledge, because in life there are many situations where knowledge fails but behavior can still handle."

The Reflection

Jim sat in his office three days after leaving Bill's dealership. The afternoon light was fading again—that same quiet hour he loved. But something had shifted in him. The question he'd carried into Chapter 2 had evolved.

Before, he'd asked: How do I hand off a way of thinking? Now he was asking: What systems must be in place for that way of thinking to survive and scale? Zip codes had been a revelation. Not because they were new—they'd existed since 1963—but because Jim had witnessed Bill use them as a lens, not just a tool.

Geography revealed behavior—behavior-informed decisions. The sequence was clean. The logic was sound.

But as Jim reviewed his notes, he kept coming back to one moment. Bill had said something almost in passing: "Most people use this every day and never realize what it really is."

That line haunted Jim.

Tools were easy to teach. A spreadsheet, a dashboard, a formula—anyone with basic training could use them. But the discipline to use tools correctly? The willingness to let data reshape intuition instead of bending intuition to defend old assumptions?

That was something else entirely.

Jim thought about his own journey. He'd been in business for forty years. Instinct had carried him far. Thousands of decisions made on a gut feel turned out right. But there were also decisions made on preference that turned out wrong—and he'd only discovered the mistakes years later, sometimes too late to correct course.

How many decisions was he still making on preference instead of evidence?

And more pressing: how could he build a company that didn't require him to be present for every decision? How could he create systems that would guide people to make good choices even when he wasn't in the room?

That was the real succession challenge.

His phone rang. Jim picks up hearing John ask, "How was Bill's meeting?"

"Profound," Jim said. "He's teaching them to see. But I'm realizing that seeing alone isn't enough."

John understood immediately. "You're thinking about

systems." "I am."
"There's someone you need to meet," John said. "Bob. He runs one of the largest truck operations in the state. He's not famous—you won't read about him in business magazines. But he's built something that runs without him. And he did it through systems."

Jim wrote down the address.

"Bob's different from Bill," John continued. "Bill taught you to see clearly. Bob's going to teach you how to organize what you see. How to build systems that turn insight into action, automatically."

After they hung up, Jim sat with John's words. *Organize what you see. Automatically.*
That was the missing piece.

The Drive Out

The next morning, Jim left early.

The landscape changed as he drove—less congestion, more open land, fewer distractions. Urban gave way to suburban, suburban to rural. The highways widened. Traffic thinned. By the time Jim left the main highway and turned onto a county road, he was clearly in a different world.

This was truck country.

The dealership appeared gradually—first a massive lot visible from a quarter-mile away, then as he drew closer, the scale became undeniable. Trucks. Everywhere. Not just a few rows neatly arranged. Hundreds of them. Heavy-duty work trucks lined the property's front, organized by size and capacity. Pickup trucks filled entire sections—specialty vehicles— dumps, flatbeds, utility rigs—occupied their own areas.

This wasn't overstock. Jim could sense that immediately.

This was precision.

It was an intention made visible.

Bob met Jim in the parking lot. He was tall, weathered, unmistakable in his cowboy hat. His handshake was firm, his greeting warm but direct.

"Welcome to God's country," Bob said. "Largest truck selection in the state. We sell more trucks than anyone else—and not by accident."

As they walked the lot, Bob pointed out details Jim might have missed. The trucks weren't randomly positioned. Each section represented a specific market segment: work trucks for contractors, family trucks for farmers, luxury trucks for professionals, specialty vehicles for commercial fleets.

"See how we've organized the lot?" Bob asked. "Every customer who drives in knows exactly where to look. A contractor knows his trucks are in that section. A farmer knows where to find his. A family looking for a weekend vehicle knows that corner over there."

Bob gestured as he spoke. "That's not just logistics. That's customer psychology. That's respecting people's time. That's saying, 'We know who you are and what you need.'"

Jim understood. This was zip code intelligence applied to physical space.

A Culture That Wears It

Inside the dealership, Jim noticed something else immediately. Employees and customers alike wore matching cowboy hats. Not just leadership. Not just salespeople. Service techs, office staff, and even the receptionist.

This wasn't branding in the traditional sense. It was belonging.

Jim had learned through forty years of studying dealerships that culture couldn't be forced. It either emerged from alignment between values, systems, and behavior—or it was theater. Matching hats could have been theater.

But watching how people moved through the building, how they greeted each other, how they treated customers—this was genuine. The hats were a symbol of something real.

Bob caught Jim observing and smiled. "Culture is a system too," Bob said. "Most leaders think culture is a feeling. It's not. It's the result of aligned systems."

They climbed the stairs to the conference room. On the way up, Jim noticed another detail. Above the sales floor, a sign hung in large letters:

If you can't measure it, you can't manage it.

Jim smiled to himself. Decades earlier, in his radio days, the sign above his own desk had read: "A dollar for a holler." Back then, energy mattered more than accuracy. Enthusiasm was the currency.

Now, accuracy was the energy. Times had changed.

The Whiteboard Reveals Structure

Bob's team had gathered in the conference room. About fifteen people— sales managers, a finance director, a general manager, the service director, and a few others Jim didn't immediately identify.

On the whiteboard, someone had written:

THE TRANSITION

From Gut Instinct to Data-Driven Leadership

Below that, five lines:

- Experience creates instinct
- Instinct shapes questions
- Data tests assumptions
- Technology scales execution
- Measurement drives learning

Bob pointed to the board.

"We didn't abandon instinct," he said, looking directly at Jim. "We organized it. We turned it from something private—something only in my head—into something systematic. Something that survives me."

That line stayed with Jim immediately. Turn it from something private into something systematic.

That was the answer to the succession question. Not eliminating intuition, organizing it, and making it teachable and repeatable.

The Framework Made Visible

Bob gestured for Jim to step forward. He stood and walked to the whiteboard. For years, he'd carried a framework in his mind but had never formally laid it out.

This seemed like the moment.

He picked up the marker and drew a vertical structure:

THE ALIGNMENT FRAMEWORK

1. Instinct — Earned through experience
2. Systems — Built for consistency
3. Data — Reveals reality
4. Technology — Accelerates execution
5. Measurement — Creates feedback loops

Jim stepped back and looked at what he'd written. "Most organizations jump straight to number four," he continued. "They see competitors using new technology. They see vendors promising automation. They buy the tool first and try to build the rest around it."

Jim tapped the board at *Technology*.

"That's why most technology investments fail. That's why you hear leaders say, 'We spent $500,000 on software, and it hasn't changed anything.' They skipped steps one through three."

Bob nodded slowly. His team was utterly silent, present. "You can't automate clarity," Jim continued. "You have to build clarity first. Instinct has to come first—earned experience, pattern recognition, the accumulated wisdom of people who've actually done the work."

Jim tapped *Instinct.*

"From there, you build systems. Not to replace instinct, but to organize it. To make it visible. To make it teachable. To make it repeatable."

He moved to *Systems.*

"Once instinct is organized into systems, then you bring in data. Data tests your assumptions. Data says, 'Your instinct was right about X, but you were wrong about Y.' Data is the reality check."

He tapped *Data.*

"Only after instinct is organized and data is informing decisions do you add technology. Technology amplifies what's already working. If what's working isn't clear,

technology just makes the dysfunction bigger and faster."
Jim looked at the room, continuing, "And finally, measurement. Not to judge people. Not to create scorecards. But to close the loop. Measurement shows us what's working, what's not, and where we need to adjust. Measurement is how we stay curious instead of confident."

Jim put the marker down. "The leaders who endure," he said, "aren't the ones chasing the shiniest new tool. They're the ones who understand this sequence. They build methodically, from instinct to systems to data to technology to measurement. Each one prepares the ground for the next."
Bob smiled. "That's exactly what we've done here. That's why we've survived three recessions. That's why we're still growing when competitors are struggling."

From Gut to Organization

Later, with the two seated in Bob's office, Jim listened as Bob explained how his transition unfolded.

"Twenty years ago, I ran this place on instinct," Bob said. "I knew trucks. I knew what customers wanted. I could walk a lot and tell you what would sell just by looking at the inventory. My gut was good."

Bob leaned back in his chair, explaining, "But my gut couldn't run two locations. And it definitely couldn't run five. I'd clone myself into exhaustion, and nothing still felt quite right at the other branches."

Bob stood and walked to a shelf. He pulled down a thick binder labeled "2005."

"That's when I realized I had to get out of my own head," Bob said. "I had to take what I knew—the thousands of small decisions I made automatically— and make them explicit. Write them down. Share them. Build them into processes."

He opened the binder. Jim saw inventory guidelines, customer profiles, seasonal strategies, and staffing models.

"It took two years to codify what was in my head," Bob described. "And you know what? Some of it was wrong. Once I wrote it down, once other people saw it, I discovered that some of my 'instinct' was actually just habit. Some of it was outdated. Some of it was brilliant." Bob closed the binder, clarifying, "Once I separated the brilliant from the habitual, I could scale. I could hire general managers who understood the principle, not just took orders. I could let them make decisions that felt aligned even when I wasn't in the room."

Jim understood immediately. Systems weren't restrictions. Systems were freedom. Freedom to let good people make good decisions—freedom to scale without the founder being the bottleneck.

"That's succession," Jim said. "Right there."

Bob nodded. "It's the only kind of succession that works. You don't leave a business. You leave a way of thinking. And the way of thinking only survives if it's been organized into systems."

GRP Still Works (But It's Evolved)

Bob then shifted gears. He stood and moved to another part of the whiteboard. Someone had written:

GRP = Reach × Frequency

"This is the oldest formula in media planning," Bob said. "Gross Rating Points. You need enough people to see your message enough times to change behavior. That's it. That's the math."

He looked at Jim. "Nothing's changed about this formula," Bob said. "Whether it's television, streaming, digital video, audio, social—the math is still true. Reach times Frequency still equals impact."

Jim nodded. He'd known this intellectually, but hearing Bob say it—with conviction, from someone running a massive operation—brought clarity.

"But what has changed is visibility," Bob continued. "Technology used to hide these metrics. You'd run a TV campaign and hope it was reaching people. You'd count cars on the lot and figure out roughly what was working."

Bob gestured around the room. "Now, technology lets us see exactly what's happening. We can measure exposure at the household level. We can analyze frequency saturation by ZIP Code. We can track lift across channels in near-real time. We can adjust creative, timing, and spend dynamically based on what the data is telling us."

He paused, then continued, "But the fundamental principle hasn't changed. Reach. Frequency. Behavior change. That's still the formula."

Bob then showed the group how this applied across his

own operation. He displayed a dashboard that showed:

- Which zip codes were being reached most frequently
- Which messages resonated in which neighborhoods
- How frequency saturation affected response rates
- Where diminishing returns set in
- When to shift budget to new audiences

"This is GRP applied to reality," Bob said. "This is instinct organized through systems, informed by data, amplified by technology, and measured relentlessly."

Jim saw it clearly now. It wasn't a new formula. It was an old formula made visible.

The Universal Bridge

Bob then did something that deeply impressed Jim. He brought out case studies from entirely different industries.

"I spent time with a hospital administrator who used the

same principles," Bob said. "She had three emergency rooms. One was always backed up. The other two had wait times. Seemed random."

Bob pulled up a one-page summary, explaining, "She mapped patient arrival patterns—location, time of day, severity of condition. Same principle as zip codes. Different data. She discovered that patients from certain zip codes arrived in clusters. By adjusting staffing patterns to match arrival patterns, she reduced wait times by 40 percent."

Jim leaned forward.

"Same principle," Bob continued. "See clearly. Understand patterns. Build systems. Measure results." Bob showed another example—a financial services company managing risk. Another—a manufacturer optimizing inventory. Another—a technology startup scaling culture.

"Different industries," Bob said. "Same discipline. The leaders who endure don't rely on gut alone. And they don't surrender judgment to algorithms. They guide technology with experience."

Jim saw it now. This wasn't a truck dealership secret. This was a leadership principle that worked everywhere.

The Succession Moment

As the meeting continued, Jim watched something meaningful happen. One of Bob's sons—probably in his late twenties—asked how to apply the framework when the data was unclear.

Bob paused. Instead of answering immediately, he turned to the group.

"This is the question," Bob said. "When do you trust the data? When do you trust instinct?"

The room engaged. Different perspectives emerged. Someone suggested thresholds—"Trust data when you have three months of consistent results." Someone else pushed back—"But markets shift faster than that now."

Bob let them debate, then he spoke: "You trust data more than instinct, but not absolutely. You use data to question instinct. You use instinct to interpret data. Neither alone. Always together."

Jim realized what was happening. Bob was teaching his son not just how to use the framework, but how to think about the framework. How to stay curious. How to avoid becoming dogmatic about any single tool or principle.

This was preparation. This was succession done right.

After the meeting ended and most of the team had left, Bob's son stayed behind.

"I want to do things differently from you," he said to Bob. "New approaches. Different channels. Faster iteration."

Bob smiled. "Good. I hope you do. But use the same framework to think about it. See clearly. Organize your instinct. Test with data. Scale with technology. Measure relentlessly. Do all that, and you can change everything else, and it'll still work."

Jim felt something shift in his own thinking. Succession wasn't about preserving the past. It was about giving the next generation a framework flexible enough to adapt while holding enough structure not to lose the plot.

Jim's Field Notes — The Alignment Questions

As the afternoon deepened, Bob gave Jim a handwritten list of questions he asked whenever new initiatives were proposed:

Where are we making decisions based on comfort instead of evidence?
Where is data available but ignored?
Where has technology been added without redesigning systems?
Which metrics inform learning—and which merely report outcomes?
Are we measuring inputs (activities) or outputs (results)?

Do our people understand the principle, or just the tactic?

Jim read through the list and realized these questions applied equally to a dealership, a marketing agency, a hospital, a nonprofit, a family business, or a startup.

The Drive Home

Driving home that evening, Jim reflected on what he'd witnessed.

The truck lot. The organized inventory. The matching hats. The whiteboard framework. The dashboard. The father-son conversation.

None of it was flashy.

None of it would have made a good LinkedIn post or a viral TikTok. But it was all real. It was all built on principle. It was all designed to survive without Bob personally driving every decision.

Bob had taken his instinct—earned through decades of

experience—and organized it into systems. Those systems had then been informed by data, amplified by technology, and refined through measurement.

And because he'd done that methodically, he could hand it to the next generation in a way that didn't require them to become him. They could become themselves while staying true to the framework.

Jim thought back to Chapter 1. The succession question. What happens to a mission when the founder leaves?

Bob's answer was clear: it survives if it's been systematized. And it thrives if the systems are flexible enough to evolve.

As Jim drove through the evening, one more clarity emerged. This wasn't really about marketing anymore. This wasn't about zip codes or GRPs or dashboards.
It was about leadership in a world where intuition alone could no longer keep pace with complexity.

The leaders of the past could rely on gut instinct and personal relationships.

The leaders of the future would need something more: systems that organized intuition, made it teachable, and survived transitions.

The Second Pillar Emerges

That night, Jim sat at his desk and added another entry to his framework.

The first pillar had been: *See the Market Clearly Before You Act*

The second pillar was becoming clear: *Build Systems That Align Reality to Intention*

Not systems for control. Not systems that stifled innovation. But systems that:

- Organized instinct without eliminating it
- Made thinking visible so it could be taught
- Created consistency without requiring clones
- Allowed measurement without creating fear
- Provided structure while inviting adaptation

Jim wrote one sentence in his notebook that night:

When instinct is aligned with systems, and systems are amplified by technology, leadership becomes scalable. And more than that, it became teachable. It became heritable.

It became the kind of legacy that could survive the founder's leaving.

Jim closed his notebook and sat back in his chair. The office was quiet again. The afternoon light had given

way to evening.

Two chapters down. Many more to go. But the

framework was taking shape.

See clearly.

Build systems.

The next pillar—measurement, reflection, and the disciplines of learning— would follow.

And Jim knew from his conversation with John that there were still other mentors waiting, different lessons to be learned, other ways of thinking to discover.

But tonight, he understood something fundamental: The greatest gift a leader could leave wasn't a business. It was a way of thinking about business.

The greatest responsibility was making sure that the way of thinking survived the founder's departure.

Bob had done that, Bill had done that, and John was trying to do that.

And Jim's job—in writing this book, in documenting these lessons, in sharing these frameworks—was to help leaders everywhere do the same.

"Planning your media 90 days out prevents panic. Commitment prevents chaos."

Ad Man Notes – Key Principles:

Lesson 1: Instinct Must Be Organized to Scale. Great intuition trapped in one person's head becomes a bottleneck. Systems make instinct teachable and repeatable.

Lesson 2: Technology Amplifies Whatever Already Exists. If systems are unclear, technology accelerates dysfunction. If systems are aligned, technology multiplies impact.

Lesson 3: Succession Only Works When Thinking Is Systematized.

You don't replace founders — you preserve frameworks that allow others to lead without becoming clones.

YOUR KEY NOTES

PILLARS OF LEADERSHIP

THE FRAMEWORK FOR LONGEVITY IN AUTOMOTIVE

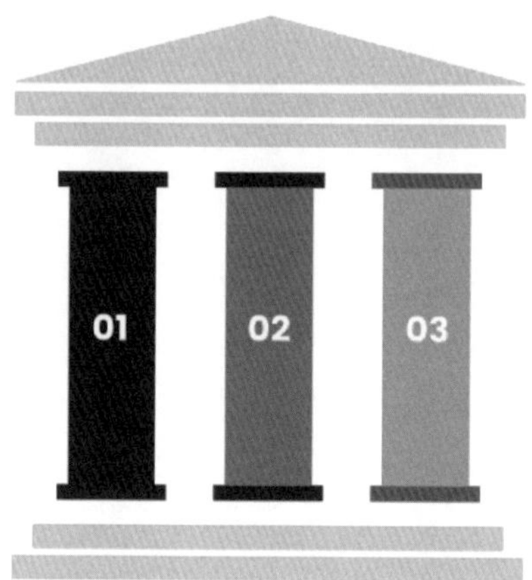

See the Market Clearly Before You Act

Understand Customer Behavior Through Patterns

Measure Daily and Adjust Constantly

Chapter 4

Measure Twice, Scale Once

"Measure twice, cut once is always the best rule."

The Unexpected Summons

Jim didn't expect the call—but the tone told him everything. "Jim, my name is Fred Sr. I'm a friend of John's. I'd like you to come see me tomorrow. My son Freddy Jr. will pick you up in our plane. Eight a.m. sharp. Don't worry— he'll have you back tomorrow night."

The line went dead before Jim could respond, a smile tugging on his lips. People who spoke that way usually had something worth learning.

It had been three weeks since his conversation with John about zip codes. Three weeks of sitting with the idea, turning it over in his mind, wondering how deep it really went. Three weeks of reviewing notes, watching videos of whiteboard sessions, and reading the statistics John had sent over.

But something was still missing.

Jim had learned to see clearly. That was John's gift—the discipline of looking at markets the way they actually were, not the way dealers wished them to be. But seeing clearly and acting decisively were two different things. How did a dealer turn sight into a system? How did Fred Sr. build an organization where everyone moved with the same intuition, even when he wasn't in the room?

That, Jim suspected, was what this visit was really about.

The Lesson Begins Before the Lesson

Freddy Jr. was waiting exactly where he said he'd be. The plane was spotless—painted in a red, white, and blue scheme that felt deliberate rather than decorative.

As they climbed, Jim asked the obvious question. "Did your dad say what today's meeting is about?"

Freddy Jr. grinned. "It's always the same thing." He paused, then said, "Measuring."

Jim raised an eyebrow.

Freddy Jr. laughed. "He says, 'Measure twice, cut once.' He has my whole life. You want to know something funny? I didn't really understand what it meant until I was in my twenties. Turns out it's not about carpentry at all."

"What's it about?" Jim asked.

"Discipline," Freddy Jr. said. "The discipline to know before you act. The discipline to measure reality instead of guessing it. The discipline to let data reshape your thinking instead of using data to defend what you already believe."

Jim leaned back. He'd spent forty years working with dealers who chased the next idea, the next promotion, the next shiny tactic. Very few led with discipline. Most led with energy. In dealerships, enthusiasm was the currency—the louder you shouted, the faster you moved, the more you seemed to know.

This trip was already different.

Freddy Jr. continued. "My dad would tell you that measurement is boring. That's how you know it works. It's not exciting. It's not a secret. It's just discipline applied daily until it becomes culture."

The plane leveled off. Below them, Iowa stretched out in a patchwork of fields, roads, and small towns.

Where Culture Shows Itself

As they landed, Jim noticed a man standing near the hangar doors. The moment the plane stopped, two attendants rushed forward, chocked the wheels, and opened the door.

"Welcome. Fred's right there."

Fred Sr. moved with purpose—confident, efficient. He shook Jim's hand, complimented Freddy Jr.'s flying, then laughed, "I taught him everything he knows. Truth is, he's better than I ever was—but don't tell him that."

Freddy Jr. heard it anyway. He smiled.

Jim noticed something immediately: This wasn't a dealership built on ego. It was built on process and trust.

They drove to the dealership in comfortable silence. Not the awkward silence of strangers, but the kind that comes from people who don't need to fill space with words because the work speaks for itself.

The Room That Told the Truth

The conference room was full, the front row conspicuously empty. Fred Sr. waved Jim and Freddy Jr. forward. Freddy Jr. stepped up, scanned the room, and said, “Today, we’re going to talk about my favorite subject.”

Without hesitation, the room answered in unison: "Measurements."

The laughter wasn't forced. It was familiar. The kind of familiarity that comes from hearing the same message so many times that it becomes the soundtrack of a company.

Jim leaned toward Fred Sr. "You trained them well."

Fred Sr. shook his head. "I trained the system. The system trained them."

That sentence stayed with Jim.

It was the opposite of what most dealers did. Most dealers built around individuals—the best salesperson, the sharpest sales manager, the sharpest finance person.

When those people left, the business suffered. But Fred Sr. had built something different. He'd built infrastructure. A system so clear, so visible, so grounded in daily measurement that any competent person could step into it and produce results.

That was the real succession secret.

Backward Is the Only Way Forward

Fred Sr. went to the whiteboard. "Every month starts with one number," he said. "Units sold."

He wrote: *Target: 300 Units*

"Our close ratio is eighteen percent," Fred Sr. continued. "That means we need 1,680 opportunities—ups—every month."

Jim nodded. This wasn't a theory. This was math. Cold, clean, undeniable math.

"To get that traffic," Fred Sr. continued, "we need 1,800 GRPs."

He paused and looked at the room, joking, "And before anyone asks—yes, we know exactly what that costs."

He then wrote: $100,000–$120,000 per month

Jim stepped in. "Most dealers your size wouldn't spend that."

Fred Sr. smiled. "Most dealers my size don't know what

their market actually does. They spend money because they've always spent money. Or they cut spending because times got tight. They never actually connect the dots between what they spend and what they get."

A hand went up from the back of the room. A finance director, Jim guessed, but she asked, "What if our close ratio drops to sixteen percent?"

Fred Sr. turned to the whiteboard without hesitation. "Then we need 1,875 ups. Which means we need 1,950 GRPs. Which costs us about $130,000 per month—unless we shift budget to higher-converting zip codes."

He drew an arrow on the board, pointing backward from the final number to each preceding step. "This is how we think - we start with the goal. We work backward to the inputs. We measure everything in between."

Jim watched the room. No confusion. No anxiety. They'd had this conversation before. They understood the logic. More importantly, they understood their role in executing it.

"A lot of dealers ask me what our secret is," Fred Sr. said, looking directly at Jim. "They think it's some hidden formula. Some brilliant tactic. Something they haven't discovered yet. But there is no secret. The secret is that there is no secret. We just measure what matters. Every day. And we adjust based on what the measurements tell us."

ZIP Codes Changed Everything

Fred Sr. erased part of the board and drew a rough map of the region. "Here's where it gets interesting," he said.

"We don't treat this as one market."

Jim leaned forward. John had mentioned zip codes before, but in this setting, with the whole dealership watching, the idea carried new weight.

Fred Sr. pointed to clusters on the map. "We break our entire trading area down by zip code. And we don't do this to be fancy or complicated. We do it because it reveals the truth about our market."

He filled in the board with data points:

- Which zip codes generate the most ups

- Which converts the highest

- Which purchase new vs. used

- Which respond to TV, radio, digital, or direct mail

- Which requires frequency versus reach

- Which are growth markets and which are declining

"Zip codes aren't geography," Fred Sr. said. "They're *behavior.*"

He brought up a color-coded map on the screen—greens and blues for top performers, yellows and oranges for middle performers, and red for lagging areas.

"This green area here—52320—that's our best market. Highest traffic volume. Highest close ratio. Highest average sale price. If we're going to invest dollars, we start here."

He pointed to an orange area. "This zip code—50132—we're probably losing money trying to reach it. We've been heavy there for three years. The traffic never converts. So we're testing a lower-frequency approach. See if less investment produces the same outcome."

Jim jumped in. "So you're not buying media broadly—you're buying it *intentionally.*"

Fred Sr. nodded. "Exactly. Same total spend. Different precision." He explained that some zip codes required heavy frequency to stay top of mind because multiple competitors operated there. Other zip codes only needed light reinforcement because loyalty was strong and repeat business was consistent.

"Once we understood that," Fred Sr. continued, "our waste disappeared. We weren't cutting overall media spend. We were *relocating it*. Moving money from low-return zip codes to high-return zip codes. The result was more units at the same budget."

He turned to a sales manager in the third row. "Mark, remind Jim what happened after we implemented zip code targeting two years ago."

Mark stood up immediately. No hesitation. No papers to shuffle. Just words. "Units went from 240 to 300 a month—same ad spend. Better targeting. Better results."

Jim nodded. That was a 25% increase in volume without increasing the budget. In retail, that was the Holy Grail.

From Measurement to Market Intelligence

Jim asked the question he knew readers would be asking.

"How long did this take you to figure out?"

Fred Sr. didn't hesitate, "Years—until we made it systematic. Months ago, we did."

He explained the journey. In the beginning, zip code data was collected manually. Every night, after closing, someone logged the numbers:

- Daily ups by zip code

- Sales by zip code

- Media exposure by zip code

- Historical comparisons year-over-year

- Conversion rates

- Average sale price per zip code

"It was tedious," Fred Sr. said. "Literally spreadsheet work every single night. But the moment we started *looking* at the data—really looking at it, not just skimming it—patterns emerged that we never would have seen otherwise."

He told a story. Two years into measuring by zip code, Fred Sr. noticed something odd. Zip code 50322—one of his strongest markets—had started to decline. Gradually at first. Then more noticeably.

"I could have ignored it," Fred Sr. admitted. "The overall store numbers were still strong. But I looked deeper. Traffic was down in that zip code specifically. Close ratio was down there, too. Something was changing."

He did the detective work. Turned out that a major employer in that zip code had moved most of its operations to another city. It wasn't announced publicly. But the data told the story before the newspapers did.

"So we adjusted," Fred Sr. continued. "We moved that budget to zip codes with growing employment. We expanded our reach into the suburbs where people were actually moving to. And we stayed ahead of the market shift."

He paused, then explained, "Most dealers I know would have just noticed the decline in the spreadsheet at year-end after the damage was done. By then, you've already wasted a quarter's worth of budget on media reaching people who aren't there anymore."

Jim understood. The discipline of measurement wasn't just about optimization. It was about early warning. It was about seeing market shifts before they became crises.

"What started manual is now digital," Fred Sr. said. "Dashboards, charts, visual trends. But the discipline never changed."

Jim nodded. "Technology didn't create the insight—it revealed it faster."

Fred Sr. smiled. "That's the difference between tools and systems. A tool is something you use when you think of using it. A system is something that runs automatically. We use dashboards now. But we could go back to spreadsheets tomorrow, and the system would still work because the thinking is built in."

Why Current Data Matters More Than Ever

Fred Sr. turned serious. "In the old days," he said, "we looked at monthly data. Sometimes quarterly data. We'd wait until the numbers were in, analyze them, make decisions, execute, and hope we were right."

He pointed to a chart on the screen. "Now we look at daily data. Sometimes, there is hourly data on traffic numbers. Real-time is the new baseline."

He outlined why real-time measurement mattered:

- Predictive models require fresh inputs. Stale data predicts the past, not the future.

- Market behavior shifts faster than annual plans. Three months ago, gas prices spiked. What was your market response? Did you measure it daily or monthly?

- Zip-level changes reveal early opportunity and risk before they show up at the store level.

- Leading indicators beat vanity metrics every time. It doesn't matter if your impressions are up if your traffic is down.

"When zip code 50322 slows before the rest of the market," Fred Sr. said, "we see it first. And we act first. That's how leaders get ahead without guessing."

He told another story. A competitor had opened a new dealership across town, targeting the same zip codes Fred Sr. serviced. Most dealers would have waited to see the damage—lower traffic, lower sales. Then they

would have panicked and overspent on reactive promotions.

"We noticed the shift in the data first," Fred Sr. said. "So instead of reacting, we got ahead of it. We increased frequency in those zip codes. We tested a new creative. We moved inventory to match what those customers were buying. When our competitor realized they were there, we'd already inoculated our market. Traffic stayed stable."

He looked at Jim. "That's what systems do. They let you respond faster because you're measuring constantly."

The Dealer-to-CEO Shift

As the meeting wrapped up, Fred Sr. asked Jim if he wanted to say anything to the team.

Jim stood up. He'd been sitting there for hours, watching, listening, understanding. "A dealer runs on instinct," he said. "He walks the lot. He talks to the customers. He feels what's working. He's got good instincts because he's been doing this for twenty, thirty, forty years. That instinct is valuable."

He paused, then admitted, "But a CEO builds systems so instinct becomes optional. So the business doesn't rely on whether one person is having a good day. So anyone—anyone competent—can step into the role and produce

consistent results."

He looked to Fred Sr. “This place isn’t dependent on Fred Sr. It’s dependent on the system—zip code targeting, daily measurement, backward planning from units to GRPs to budget. Who’s in charge doesn’t matter. The system works.”

Fred Sr. nodded. "Instinct is earned. Systems protect it."

That was the bridge.

Jim wasn't there to replace Fred Sr.'s expertise. He was there to translate it into leadership thinking. To take what a brilliant dealer had intuited and turn it into infrastructure that could survive any transition.

The Measurement-to-Scale Framework. On the flight home, Jim wrote down what he'd observed. Not just the zip code system, but the deeper principle underneath it.

He sketched a framework:

The Growth Alignment Framework

1. Measure (Reality)

- Units sold

- Close ratios

- Traffic (ups)

- Spend efficiency

- Zip code performance

- Real-time data feeds

⬇

2. Segment (Behavior)

- Zip code clusters
- Media responsiveness
- Purchase patterns
- Frequency vs. reach needs
- Declining vs. growth markets

⬇

3. Model (Prediction)

- GRPs → Traffic → Sales relationship
- Budget forecasting
- Market expansion scenarios
- Early warning indicators
- Competitive response planning

⬇

4. Systemize (Consistency)

- Dashboards

- Automated reporting

- Performance thresholds

- Accountability loops

- Decision frameworks

⬇

5. Scale (Freedom)

- Confident investment

- Reduced waste

- Leadership leverage

- Predictable growth

- Scalable succession

Each level depended on the one before it. You couldn't build a predictive model without data. You couldn't understand behavior without data. You couldn't create a system without understanding behavior. You couldn't scale without systems in place.

The Third Pillar Emerges

That night, Jim added to his notes:

The first pillar had been*: See the Market Clearly Before You Act*

The second had been: *Understand Customer Behavior Through Patterns*

The third pillar was now clear: *Measure Daily and Adjust Constantly*

But it was bigger than just measurement. It was about using measurement as the language of leadership. Fred Sr. didn't talk to his team through intuition or authority. He spoke through data. Numbers. Clear, indisputable facts about what was working and what wasn't.

Jim wrote one sentence in his notebook:

Measurement creates visibility. Visibility creates models. Models create freedom.

This chapter wasn't about advertising. It wasn't even about zip codes, though zip codes had been the revelation.

It was about control without micromanagement. About building an organization where every person understood the goal, understood what mattered, and understood how their work connected to results.

It was about the kind of leadership that could survive the founder. Jim's field notes—The questions Fred Sr. asked every day.

Before leaving the dealership, Fred Sr. handed Jim a one-page document. It was creased and worn, clearly printed and used dozens of times.

The Daily Measurement Questions

What did traffic look like by zip code yesterday?

Which zip codes are outperforming their targets? Which are underperforming?

Is there a pattern? Is the problem market-wide or zip-specific?

What's our media doing in underperforming zip codes? Are we reaching the right people? Is our message working?

What's our close ratio trend? By zip code? By product (new vs. used)?

Are there early warning indicators (declining traffic before declining sales) that we're missing?

What happened with our major competitor? Did anything change in their media, pricing, or inventory?

Are we being precise with our budget, or are we hoping our way through the month?

Jim read through the list. The questions were simple. They weren't complicated. They didn't require advanced analytics or data science. But they required daily discipline.

They required asking the same questions, studying the same metrics, tracking the same trends—day after day, month after month, year after year—until the answers became instinctive.

That was the real measurement system. Not the technology. Not the dashboards. But the discipline of asking the right questions daily and acting on what you find.

The Drive Home

Driving to the airport for his flight back, Jim thought about what he'd witnessed.

Fred Sr. wasn't a marketing genius. He wasn't a technologist. He was a dealer who had learned one thing and practiced it relentlessly: Measure what matters—

every day. Let the data tell you where to go next.

That simplicity was powerful. Because it wasn't about being right, it was about being responsive.

Fred Sr. didn't have to predict the future perfectly. He just had to notice market shifts faster than his competition and adjust faster.

Zip codes had been the tool. Measurement was the discipline. Systems were the result.

And the result was a dealership that didn't depend on one person. That could scale. That could transition. That would survive.

Jim understood now what his conversations with John had been missing.

Seeing the market clearly was essential. But seeing wasn't enough. You had to measure what you saw. You had to turn observation into data. You had to create systems around that data. And you had to trust the system more than you trusted your gut.

That was the bridge from founder-led to system-led.

That was real succession.

Central Takeaway

If you can't measure behavior by market, you can't scale performance. Zip codes turn intuition into infrastructure. Measurement turns hope into evidence. Daily discipline turns a business into a system that survives the founder.

That's what Fred Sr. taught Jim.

And that's what leaders need to understand: The greatest competitive advantage isn't a brilliant idea. It's the discipline to measure, notice, and respond faster than anyone else.

That's how you scale.

That's how you lead without being there.

That's how you create something that will outlast you.

End Quote: *"Hope is not a strategy. Measurement is."*

Ad Man Notes – Key Principles:

Lesson 1: Measurement Is for Learning, Not Judgment Metrics should inform better decisions, not punish people. Fear-based measurement kills innovation.

Lesson 2: Scaling Too Early Locks in Mistakes Leaders who rush to scale without validation institutionalize inefficiency.

Lesson 3: Precision Beats Speed Slower, deliberate measurement upfront creates faster growth over time.

YOUR KEY NOTES

1. Dashboards show reality
2. Models Predict Outcomes
3. Automation Acts Early
4. Humans Apply Judgement

Chapter 5

When Systems Start Thinking

"A system is never the sum of its parts; it is the product of their interaction." Ackoff

Jim had learned something critical from Bill.

Measurement created clarity.

But clarity alone did not create momentum.

The businesses that stalled weren't blind—they were informed. Dashboards glowed. Reports stacked up. Meetings multiplied. And yet decisions still lagged behind reality.

Jim had seen it too many times.

Seeing the truth is not the same as acting on it.

That realization framed Jim's next assignment.

From Visibility to Velocity

Auto World didn't feel like a dealership—it felt like a command center. Five franchises. One campus. Thousands of daily decisions are happening without friction.

Larry, the man behind it all, opened the meeting not with technology, but with history. "My father started this business with index cards," he said. "Names. Birthdays. Families. Notes."

Jim smiled. He'd heard this story before—in different industries, different decades, always with the same lesson.

Great systems don't begin with software.

They begin with respect for people.

Identity Before Infrastructure

Larry advanced the slide:

IDENTITY IS EVERYTHING

Proximity, not just presence

Jim leaned forward. “Most companies,” he continued, “know where their customers live. Very few understand how people in those places behave.”

Zip codes weren’t geography. They were *behavioral shortcuts*. People clustered by zip code tend to:

· Consume similar media

· Respond to messaging at similar frequencies

· Share life stages and income bands

·Move through buying cycles in predictable rhythms

Zip codes compress thousands of individual variables into a usable signal. Jim put it simply:

"Zip codes don't tell you who someone is. They tell you how people like them tend to act."

That was the bridge—from raw data to intelligence.

Why Dashboards Alone Stall Progress

Larry gestured toward the dashboards lining the back wall. "We had all of this," he said. "Before we had momentum."

Jim nodded.

Dashboards create visibility, not velocity.

They:

- Show what happened
- Require interpretation
- Depend on meetings
- Move at human speed

And worst of all, they create the illusion of control.

Jim addressed the room. “If your system waits for a meeting to respond,” he said, “you’re already late.”

Dashboards stall progress when:

· No thresholds trigger action

· No models suggest responses

· No automation exists

· No ownership is predefined

Visibility without response is just observation.

Diagram 1: Why Dashboards Plateau

DATA → DASHBOARD → MEETING → DECISION → ACTION

↑

DELAY

Jim let that sit. “Dashboards inform humans,” he said. “They don’t protect them from delay.”

How Models Convert Insight into Foresight

Jim shifted the conversation. “Insight tells you what happened,” he said. “Models tell you what’s likely to happen next.”

Larry advanced the slide.

Models connected relationships:

· GRPs → Traffic → Sales

· ZIP Code Frequency → Response Rate

· Service Visits → Repurchase Probability

Once relationships are modeled, systems stop reporting and start anticipating.

Jim framed it clearly:

“Insight tells the story. Models tell you the ending—unless you change it.”

That’s where leadership gains leverage.

Diagram 2: Insight vs. Foresight

INSIGHT (Dashboard):

Sales 1 in zip 50322

FORESIGHT (Model):

Engagement 1 → Service Visits 1 → Sales 1 in 30 days

Models buy time.

Time buys options.

CRMs, DMPs, and the Missing Layer

Larry paused on the next slide:

CRM 4 DMP 4 CDP

Jim stepped in. “A CRM remembers relationships,” he explained, “a DMP finds strangers. A CDP understands people—and acts.”

CRMs track interactions.

DMPs extend reach.

But CDPs unify behavior across systems and time.

CRM's answer: Who is this customer? What happened last?

CDP’s answer: What should we do—now—without waiting?

That distinction mattered.

Where Automation Adds Humanity

The concern surfaced, as it always did. “Doesn’t this remove the human element?”

Jim shook his head. “Automation doesn’t remove empathy,” he said. “It removes delay, repetition, and guesswork.”

Automation adds humanity when it:

- Ensures no customer is forgotten
- Triggers timely follow-up
- Escalates issues early

· Removes bias from routine decisions

· Frees people to listen instead of monitoring

Technology handled the predictable.

People handled the meaningful.

Diagram 3: Automation That Preserves Humanity

BEHAVIOR SIGNAL →

SYSTEM ACTION →

HUMAN INTERVENTION (WHEN IT MATTERS)

Example:

· Zip code engagement drops

· The system adjusts frequency automatically

· The manager is alerted only if the decline persists

No panic.

No overreaction.

No missed moment.

Zip Codes Meet Intelligent Systems

Jim tied it back to Chapter 4.

"When zip code behavior, CRM history, and real-time engagement live in one system," he said, "the business stops waiting."

The system could:

- Shift spend by neighborhood
- Suppress ads to recent buyers
- Route high-intent leads instantly
- Flag risk before revenue drops

This wasn't marketing automation.

It was decision automation.

Diagram 4: Zip Codes as Behavioral Shortcuts

ZIP CODE → BEHAVIOR PATTERN → MODEL → AUTOMATED RESPONSE

Zip codes reduced noise.

Models added foresight.

Automation-protected timing.

The Leadership Shift

Jim closed the session with a simple framework:

1. Dashboards show reality
2. Models predict outcomes
3. Automation acts early
4. Humans apply judgment

Technology handled stages one through three.

Leadership owned the fourth.

Chapter 5 Central Insight

Zip codes simplify behavior.

Models convert insight into foresight. Automation protects humanity.

Dashboards alone are not leadership.

Growth doesn't come from more data.

It comes from systems that act, so people don't have to chase reality.

End Quote: *"If you don't stand for something, you will fall for anything."*

Ad Man Notes – Key Principles

Lesson 1: Systems Should Reduce Cognitive Load, Not Add to It The best systems guide behavior naturally instead of forcing compliance.

Lesson 2: Automation Without Understanding Is Dangerous When systems "think," leaders must still interpret — not abdicate judgment.

Lesson 3: Discipline Creates Freedom Well-designed systems free leaders to focus on strategy instead of constant correction.

YOUR KEY NOTES

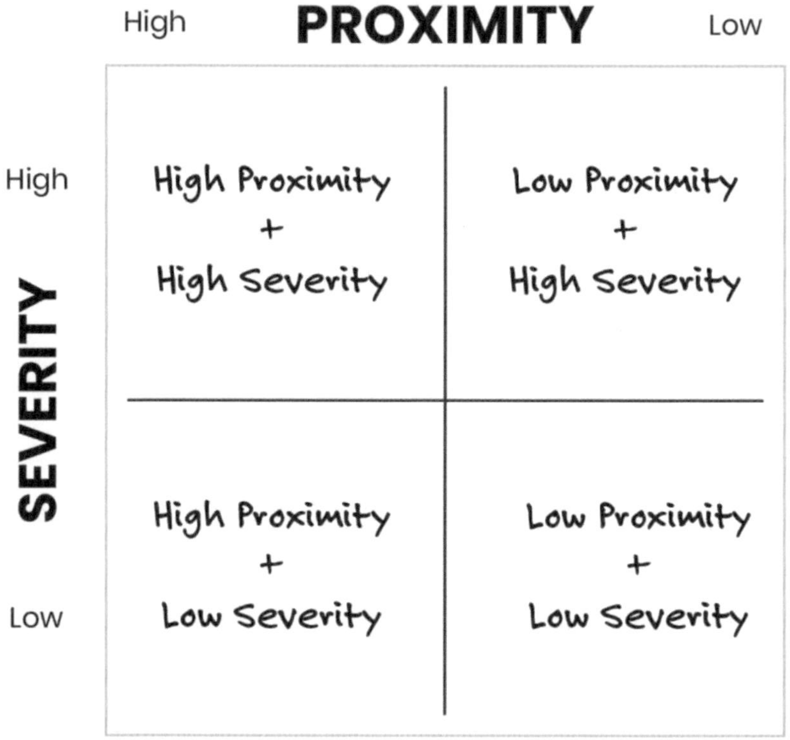

	High **PROXIMITY** Low	
SEVERITY High	High Proximity + High Severity	Low Proximity + High Severity
Low	High Proximity + Low Severity	Low Proximity + Low Severity

Chapter 6

Proximity, Not Just Severity

"Through proximity you absorb the traits, actions and beliefs of the people you associate with. Consciously and unconsciously, their knowledge and ideas become a part of who you are." Ed Mylett.

The Day Everything Was Urgent

By 8:15 a.m., the day was already off script.

A client success manager had sent a message marked URGENT. A long-time dealer had called Jim's cell twice in a row—a pattern that never meant small talk. The data team flagged an overnight identity sync issue affecting several in-flight campaigns.

None of the issues, on their own, looked catastrophic. But all of them were close.

As Jim walked past the framed promise on the wall—We love it when you succeed—he felt its weight more sharply than usual.

Significant, abstract risks were always present. They lived in strategy decks and long-range plans.

What threatened that promise most were the things happening right now.

Not just how severe a problem was.

But how near it was.

The Line Jim Kept Repeating

Over time, Jim had developed a habit of compressing experience into language people could remember.

Some of those phrases had become part of the culture:

- *People before platforms.*
- *Measure twice, scale once.*
- *Identity is everything.*

Lately, another line had joined the list—one Jim found himself repeating whenever leadership conversations started to spiral.

"It's the proximity, not the severity, that makes the problem acute."

At first, it sounded almost too simple.

But the more Jim lived with it, the more precise it became.

A massive strategic risk five years away cannot be managed the same way as a minor issue affecting clients this week.

A "minor" operational breakdown, repeated daily, could do more damage than a dramatic one-time crisis everyone rallied around.

Severity described *magnitude.*

Proximity described *timing and concentration*.

And proximity was what turned theory into urgency.

A Meeting Full of Mixed Signals

The leadership team gathered in the conference room.

On the agenda:

- A MuddVision architecture decision that would shape identity and measurement for years
- The identity sync issue that's affecting several major dealers
- A hiring gap in onboarding that's delaying launches
- A pitch from a platform rep promising "AI audience magic"
- An exploratory discussion about expansion into a

new region

Each item mattered. But they did not matter in the same way—or on the same clock.

For fifteen minutes, the discussion bounced between topics as if everything lived at the same level of urgency. Jim listened, then he raised his hand. "We're treating these as if they're the same kind of problem," he said, "They're not."

The room fell silent, all focused on what he meant. "We're good at talking about severity," Jim continued, "What we're not naming clearly enough is *proximity.*"

Two Questions That Change the Day

Jim stood and wrote two questions on the whiteboard:

How big is this if we get it wrong?

How close is this to breaking a promise right now?

"We've spent years mastering the first question," Jim said. "We know how to talk about risk— units, revenue, brand, systems. We see markets clearly. We've built systems. We measure daily. We understand identity."

He underlined the second question. "But this is what makes a problem acute. It's not only how big it is. It's how near it is to hurting someone we've already committed to."

They began sorting the agenda through that lens.

Identity sync issue
If unresolved within forty-eight hours, several dealers would see reports that didn't match reality.
Calls would come. Trust would wobble.
High proximity.

Onboarding gap
If it continued another thirty days, every new implementation would slip. Not visible today—but close enough to compound quickly.
Rising proximity.

Architecture decision

Critical, but taking an extra week to align it with their principles wouldn't break anything today.

High severity, lower proximity.

AI pitch

Interesting. No immediate commitment required.

Low proximity.

Expansion discussion

Strategically important, but no contracts or announcements yet.

High severity, low proximity.

The importance of each issue hadn't changed. Their nearness to real consequences had.

"We're not deciding what matters," Jim said, "We're deciding what's nearest to breaking a promise. That's what makes it acute."

The Proximity Grid

Jim drew two lines on the board.

A horizontal axis: Proximity (Near -> Far)
A vertical axis: Severity (Low -> High)

Four quadrants emerged. “Let’s keep this practical,” Jim said.

High Severity / High Proximity
“These are stop-everything problems. If you ignore them, real damage happens immediately.”

High Severity / Low Proximity
“These require deep, protected thinking. They matter enormously—but not at the expense of what’s breaking today.”

Low Severity / High Proximity
“Small problems that are close. If you don’t systemize them, they train the organization to live in constant friction.”

Low Severity / Low Proximity
“Curiosities and experiments. Valuable only if they don’t displace real commitments.”

They placed each agenda item on the grid, then Jim asked a more complicated question. “Now look at our calendar,” he said. “What does it say we think is most important today?”

It didn’t match the grid.

The identity issue was last.

The architecture discussion had the longest block.

The AI pitch was uninterrupted.

They weren’t prioritizing by proximity. They were prioritizing by noise. So they reordered the day.

The identity issue moved first. The onboarding gap followed. Architecture moved into protected deep-work time later in the week. The AI pitch became exploratory. Expansion shifted into strategic planning, not daily triage.

The work didn’t get smaller.

It got clearer.

How Proximity Had Been There All Along

Driving home that night, Jim realized the idea wasn't new. It had simply been unnamed.

Zip codes were proximity systems—revealing where behavior was actually happening, not where the budget wished it were happening.

Daily measurement was proximity awareness—catching shifts when they were still small and near, not after they became annual surprises.

Identity work wasn't just about who people were. It was about how near they were to a decision—lease ends, service cycles, intent signals.

Severity existed everywhere. But proximity allowed leaders to move early instead of late.

The Proximity Framework

Back at his desk, Jim added a new heading to his notebook: *The Proximity Framework*

Name the Severity

Who gets hurt if this goes wrong—clients, people, systems, trust?

Is it a one-time hit or a compounding pattern?

Name the Proximity

When does impact show up—hours, days, weeks, months?

Is the impact concentrated or isolated?

What did yesterday's measurements say about how close this really is?

Map Before You React

High severity + high proximity → Act now.

High severity + low proximity → Schedule deep work.

Low severity + high proximity → Systemize or contain.

Low severity + low proximity → Explore carefully.

Align Time With Truth

Does today's calendar reflect proximity—or whoever

spoke last?

Recheck Often

Ask daily: What moved closer since yesterday?

Jim wrote one final line beneath it:

Severity tells you how much a problem matters.

Proximity tells you when it becomes your responsibility.

The Pillar Comes In To Focus

Late that night, Jim looked again at the pillars forming the spine of the book:

See the market clearly.

Build systems that align reality to intention.

Measure daily and adjust constantly.

Identity is everything.

Then he added the next one—carefully, deliberately: Proximity, Not Just Severity, Makes the Problem Acute.

This wasn't about ignoring the long term. It was about honoring the truth that leadership happens in days and weeks—even while planning for years.

Doing the right work in the correct order. Protecting deep thinking from constant noise. Defending promises where they were closest to being tested.

Because in the end, leadership wasn't defined only by how big a problem was. It was defined by whether you recognized when it was near.

The Proximity × Severity Decision Framework

Severity tells you how much a problem matters.
Proximity tells you when it becomes acute.

The Leadership Grid

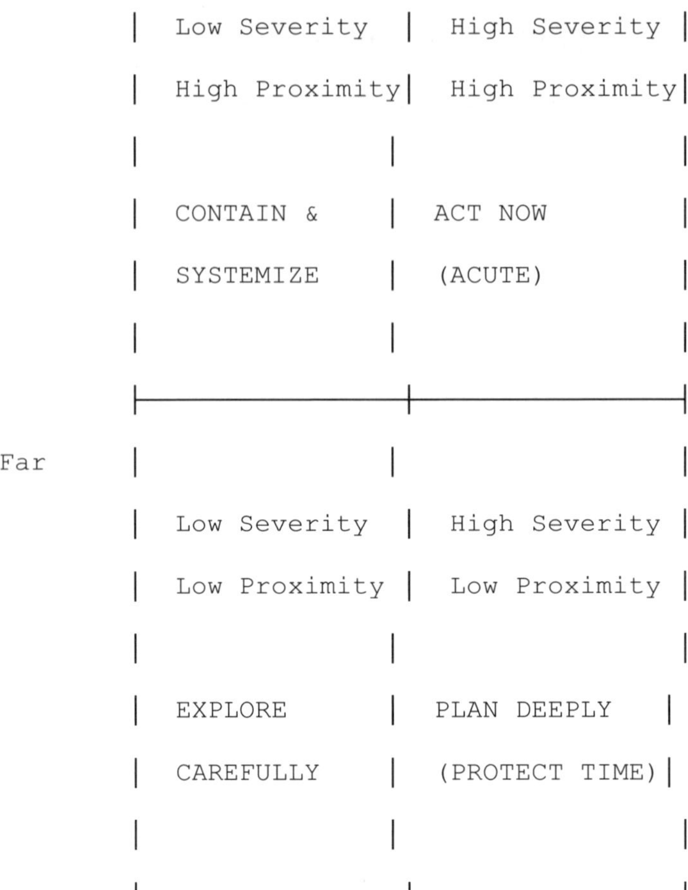

How Leaders Use the Grid

High Severity / High Proximity

→ Stop. Act. Protect promises immediately.

Examples include data integrity failures, broken client reporting, and system outages affecting live campaigns.

High Severity / Low Proximity

→ Schedule deep, uninterrupted work.

Examples include platform architecture, long-term identity strategy, and expansion planning.

Low Severity / High Proximity
→ Contain, systemize, or delegate.
Examples: repeated operational friction, manual workarounds, recurring minor errors.

Low Severity / Low Proximity
→ Experiment without distraction.
Examples: new tools, emerging ideas, and optional pilots.

The Calendar Test

If your calendar doesn't match this grid,
Your organization is being run by noise.

What the Data Quietly Confirms

Jim didn't need academic studies to believe in

proximity—but the data consistently backed him up. Across automotive, retail, and service-based organizations, the same patterns appeared:

- Issues addressed within 48 hours of the first signal were 3–5× less likely to escalate into client-facing failures.
- Data integrity issues unresolved for more than one reporting cycle increased client churn risk by 15–25%, even when overall performance remained strong
- Minor operational delays repeated weekly created more long-term dissatisfaction than single, high-visibility incidents that were resolved quickly

Severity explained the *impact.*

Proximity explained the *momentum.*

The closer a problem was to a real person—or a broken promise—the faster trust eroded.

Why Near Problems Feel Louder Than Big Ones

Jim noticed something else in the data. Problems with high proximity created cognitive load disproportionate to their size.

Leaders spent:

- More meeting time
- More emotional energy
- More reactive decision-making

On issues that were near, not necessarily large.

That wasn't a weakness.

It was biology.

Humans respond faster to what's close. Effective leaders didn't fight that instinct—they designed systems around it.

Measurement as a Proximity Sensor

Daily measurement wasn't about control.

It was about early detection.

Zip code performance, identity resolution rates, service activity, engagement drops—these weren't just metrics.

They were distance markers.

They answered one question: *How close is this to becoming real for someone else?* When measurement was reviewed weekly or monthly, proximity was already lost. When reviewed daily, leaders gained time.

And time was leverage.

Where Organizations Fail the Proximity Test

Jim had seen the same mistake repeatedly.

Teams ranked issues by:

- Revenue impact eventually
- Strategic importance in theory
- Loudness of the presenter

Instead of:

- Near-term client impact
- System integrity risk
- Promise exposure

The result wasn't a poor strategy.

It was poor sequencing.

And sequencing—not intelligence—was what separated calm organizations from chaotic ones.

Proximity Turns Strategy into Triage

Jim began to describe leadership differently.

Strategy means deciding where to go.

Proximity was the deciding factor in what to fix first so that you could get there.

Without proximity awareness:

- Big ideas crowded out urgent realities
- "Important" work displaced "necessary" work

- Teams felt busy but ineffective

With proximity awareness:

- Work aligned naturally
- Pressure decreased
- Decisions felt obvious instead of debated

Why This Became a Pillar

By the time Jim finished refining the framework, he understood why it mattered enough to stand beside the others.

Seeing the market clearly meant nothing if you couldn't tell when it moved closer. Systems failed when leaders couldn't sense pressure building near customers. Identity lost relevance when timing was ignored.

Proximity was the activator.

It turned:

- Measurement into early warning

- Identity into timely relevance
- Systems into shock absorbers instead of bottlenecks

And leadership into something calmer, steadier, and more trustworthy.

Reinforcement

Severity defines importance.

Proximity defines responsibility.

Great leaders learn to hold both at the same time—and to order their days accordingly.

"It isn't the severity, but the proximity, that makes the problem acute."

Ad Man Notes – Key Principles:

Lesson 1: Problems Feel Bigger When They're Closer

Leaders must distinguish emotional urgency from strategic importance.

Lesson 2: Not All Fires Deserve Equal Attention

Great leaders allocate energy based on impact, not noise.

Lesson 3: Distance Creates Perspective

The ability to step back emotionally improves decision quality.

YOUR KEY NOTES

Chapter 7

Technology That Serves

"Never let technology exceed humanity."

Albert Einstein

The Meeting Where the Tool Was in Charge

Jim had seen this movie before.

The conference room was packed. A vendor's laptop was already connected to the large screen. The opening slide glowed with confidence—logos, buzzwords, and a tagline promising to "transform the dealer experience through AI-powered automation."

The rep smiled as he clicked forward. “Our platform is the new standard,” he said. “To get the full value, we’ll need your team to log all activity here, adopt our reporting structure, follow our workflows, and trust our optimization engine. Once everyone’s fully onboarded, efficiency will increase dramatically.”

Jim glanced at the dealer principal. He had seen this movie before, too.

“How long does onboarding take?” the dealer asked.

“About ninety days for full adoption,” the rep replied. “We usually recommend adjusting internal processes to match our best practices. That’s how clients see the biggest gains.”

Jim listened for a few more minutes and heard the pattern he’d seen across industries. The tool wasn’t being introduced to serve the enterprise. The enterprise was being asked to reorganize itself around the tool.

When the rep paused, Jim leaned forward. “Let me make sure I understand,” he said calmly. “You’re asking this dealership to change its language, reporting cadence, and decision rhythm so it fits how your platform thinks about the world."

The rep nodded. "That's how we standardize success."

Jim smiled. "That," he said, "is exactly what we're *not* going to do."

Why Technology So Often Gets This Wrong

Jim thought about how often this mistake was made—not because leaders were careless, but because pressure distorted sequence.

Data from multiple industries told the same story:

- Over 65% of enterprise software implementations fail to deliver expected ROT within the first two years
- More than 50% of CRM and marketing automation platforms are underutilized, with fewer than half of

the core features ever adopted

- Organizations that adapt their processes to tools—rather than tools to processes—see 2– 3× higher employee friction and turnover in the first year

The pattern wasn't technical. It was philosophical.

Most organizations started with technology because:

- Competitors were buying it
- Boards wanted innovation signals
- Vendors promised speed and certainty

And only later asked how it fit who they were. Jim had learned—often the hard way—that sequence mattered more than sophistication.

You could not automate what you hadn't clarified. You could not delegate judgment to a system that didn't share your values. And you could not allow a tool to define reality for people who lived in it every day.

The Order Jim Never Compromised

Back in Bob's conference room years earlier, Jim had drawn the sequence almost without thinking. It had followed him ever since.

Instinct -> Systems -> Data -> Measurement -> Technology

Not the other way around. Instinct came first—not as gut feeling, but as lived understanding of people, markets, and consequences.

Systems translated instinct into repeatable behavior.

Data captured what systems produced.

Measurement revealed whether reality matched intention.

Technology accelerated what already worked.

When organizations inverted that order, they didn't become modern.

They became fragile.

Why MuddVision® Had to Exist

When Mudd first evaluated off-the-shelf platforms, the promises sounded familiar.

"Single source of truth."
"Unified dashboard."
"Best-practice workflows."
But every platform carried hidden assumptions:

- Geography defined by DMA instead of zip-level behavior
- Audiences owned by platforms instead of dealers
- Metrics optimized for clicks instead of units, ROs, and gross
- Identity is treated as temporary instead of compounding

If Mudd adopted those assumptions, it would slowly lose its ability to see clearly.

Once you surrender how you know the market, you

surrender leadership.

So, they did something more complex.

They built their own system—not because they wanted software, but because they wanted to protect a way of thinking.

Technology as a Hub, Not a Hero

Jim made one thing clear from the start. "MuddVision® is not the hero," he told the team. "Dealers are. Customers are. This is the hub that removes friction so the real work can happen."

Inside MuddVision®, data flowed in from everywhere that mattered:

- Media platforms via APIs (CTV, Meta, search, audio, display)
- Identity and economic data that persisted beyond cookies
- Dealer DMS and CRM feeds—ups, appointments, ROs, sales

- AI agent activity—outreach, responses, follow-up timing

What mattered wasn't volume. It was coherence.

Every signal resolved to the same household, the exact zip code, and the precise timeline of intent and action. That's what allowed the system to do something most tools never could: Connect cause to effect.

The Facts That Changed How Leaders Thought

As MuddVision® matured, the data began confirming what Jim had believed intuitively for years:

- Dealers using zip-level audience consistency across channels saw 12–20% higher close rates
- Campaigns tied to persistent household identity reduced media waste by 15–30%
- Systems that closed the loop between media, CRM, and sales reduced decision lag from weeks to days

- AI-assisted follow-up improved response speed but only when humans, not vendors, set rules

The insight was simple but profound: Technology didn't create advantage.

Alignment did.

Technology only revealed it faster.

The Leadership Principle That Completed the Arc

Late one evening, Jim sat alone in his office and reviewed the pillars that now formed a complete system:

- See the market clearly
- Build systems that align reality to intention
- Measure daily and adjust constantly
- Identity is everything
- Proximity, not just severity, makes the problem acute

Then he added the final line: *Technology must serve the way of thinking—not replace it.*

That was the end of the arc. And the beginning of succession.

Because any leader, in any industry, could apply it:

Clarify how you see the world.
Build systems that express that truth.
Use technology to accelerate—not redefine—it.

Technology Does Not Create a Legacy — It Carries One

As MuddVision® matured, Jim began to see something that went beyond performance metrics.

The real value wasn't speed.

It wasn't automation.

It wasn't even intelligence.

It was continuity.

For decades, Jim had watched businesses rise and fall not because they lacked tools, but because the thinking that built them disappeared when people changed, markets shifted, or vendors took control.

Technology, he realized, was the first tool capable of preserving a way of thinking—if it was designed correctly.

That was the line.

Technology that serves becomes a steward of legacy.

Technology that rules eventually erases it.

MuddVision® wasn't built to chase trends.

It was built to hold memory.

Memory of:

- How Mudd defined a market (zips, not abstractions)
- How identity was respected as an asset, not a

byproduct

- How measurement connected effort to outcome
- How proximity shaped decisions before damage occurred

That was legacy work.

Why Identity and Data Ownership Is Leadership, Not IT

Jim had lost count of how many times he heard the exact phrase: “That’s an IT decision.”

It was never true.

Ownership of identity and data determined:

- Who defined the customer
- Who decided what “success” looked like
- Who benefited from learning over time
- Who could change the strategy without asking

permission

Those were leadership questions, not technical ones.

Jim explained it plainly to executives: *"If you don't own identity, you don't own learning. If you don't own learning, you don't own the future."*

In many organizations:

- Platforms owned the audience
- Vendors defined the metrics
- The data was fragmented and temporary
- History disappeared when contracts ended

That wasn't modernization. It was dependency.

At Mudd, identity lived outside platforms. Households, ZIPs, VINs, service histories, and intent signals were persistent and portable.

Platforms came and went. The identity graph remained.

That decision alone:

- Reduced switching costs
- Preserved institutional memory
- Allowed AI to learn longitudinally
- Turned data into an appreciating asset

Jim saw it clearly.

Leadership is deciding what you refuse to outsource.

Identity was one of those things.

How Technology Protects Thinking Across Generations

Late one night, Jim caught himself thinking less about growth and more about durability.

What happens when I'm not in the room?

What survives when pressure hits?

What remains when tools change?

The answer wasn't a process manual. It wasn't a policy.

It wasn't even cultural slogans.

It was embedded thinking.

When systems are built around:

- Clear definitions
- Explicit priorities
- Measurable truth
- Protected identity
- Proximity-based decision rules

Then new leaders don't have to guess.

They inherit:

- How to see the market
- How to decide what matters now
- How to use technology without being shaped by it

That's how you hand thinking forward without handing control away.

Jim wrote in his notebook:

If the next generation learns only tools, it inherits fragility. If they learn frameworks, they inherit freedom.

The Test of Succession

Jim believed every system should be judged by one question:

If this technology were to disappear tomorrow, would our way of thinking still stand?

If the answer was no, the organization had confused tools with truth. MuddVision® passed that test. Not because it was perfect. But because it expressed thinking that existed before it and would exist after it.

That was *stewardship.*

The Completed Leadership Arc

By the end of Chapter 7, the arc was clear:

- Instinct without systems is fragile

- Systems without measurement are blind
- Measurement without identity is shallow
- Identity without proximity is late
- Technology without thinking is dangerous

But when aligned:

- Instinct becomes teachable
- Systems become scalable
- Measurement becomes predictive
- Identity becomes durable
- Technology becomes a servant — not a master

That was *The Ad Man 2.0.*

The Technology That Serves Scorecard

Use this scorecard before adopting, renewing, or expanding any technology.

1. Thinking Alignment

☐ Does this tool reflect how we define our market?

☐ Does it support zip-level, household-level reality?

☐ Does it reinforce our language — not replace it?

If no → Stop

2. Identity Ownership

☐ Do we own the customer identity and history?

☐ Is data portable if the tool is removed?

☐ Does learning compound over time?

If no → You are renting your future

3. System Integration

☐ Does this tool connect to our CRM, CDP, DMS, and measurement loop?

☐ Does it reduce silos instead of adding one?

☐ Does it operate as a hub or a bottleneck?

4. Automation With Humanity

☐ Does automation remove delay and repetition?

☐ Are humans still responsible for judgment and exceptions?

☐ Does it improve customer experience, not just efficiency?

5. Proximity Awareness

☐ Does the system detect what is near breaking?

☐ Are there escalation thresholds tied to time, not noise?

☐ Does it act before damage becomes visible?

6. Succession Test

☐ Could a new leader understand how to decide using this system?

☐ Does it preserve institutional memory?

☐ Would our thinking survive without it?

Final Verdict

☐ This technology serves our thinking

☐ Or we are serving the technology

Only one is acceptable.

Technology is not the Future of Leadership

Technology is the vehicle that advances leadership forward —if leaders choose wisely.

Tools do not define The Ad Man 2.0.

He is defined by:

· How he sees

· How he decides

· What he refuses to give away

· And what he builds so others can lead after him

That is not advertising.

That is stewardship.

"If the tool is in charge, leadership is already gone."

Ad Man Notes – Key Principles:

Lesson 1: Technology Is a Servant, Not a Strategy

Tools exist to support principles — never to replace them.

Lesson 2: Adoption Fails When Purpose Is Unclear

If people don't understand why technology exists, they resist it.

Lesson 3: Human Judgment Remains the Final Authority

Technology informs decisions; leaders still make them.

YOUR KEY NOTES

**"Reach tells.
Frequency *sells*.**

Chapter 8

The Enterprise Marketer's New Toolkit

"Business has only two functions – marketing and innovation."

Milan Kundera

The Question Behind the Dashboards

Jim had learned that dashboards were excellent at answering the wrong questions. Across enterprise marketing environments, platform dashboards typically optimize for:

· Reach

- Frequency
- Cost efficiency
- Engagement proxies

Yet when Jim examined enterprise outcomes across dealers and retail operators, the disconnect was consistent:

- Only 20–35% of reported "top-line marketing KPIs" had any statistically reliable relationship to revenue
- In automotive, fewer than 1 in 3 impressions delivered above a minimum threshold contributed to a showroom visit
- Click-through rate (CTR) improvements above baseline often reduced net profitability by attracting lower-intent audiences

In other words:

Platforms optimized *activity.*

Enterprises lived on *outcomes.*

That gap wasn't an execution issue—it was a measurement mismatch.

Jim's question—"Who bought the cars?"—wasn't rhetorical. It was diagnostic. If a system could not answer that question with evidence, it could not be trusted with the budget.

Why Enterprise Pain Is Structural, Not Tactical

Jim often said that enterprise marketers weren't underperforming. They were over-instrumented and under-aligned.

Across multi-location businesses, research and field data consistently showed:

- Marketing leaders touched 10–20 systems monthly
- Fewer than 30% of those systems shared data cleanly
- Decision cycles stretched 2–4× longer than market movement

- By the time reports were reviewed, behavior had already shifted

This produced a dangerous pattern:

- Meetings explained the past
- Budgets chased last month
- Learning reset instead of compounding

Jim recognized that pain wasn't solved by adding tools. It was solved by re-architecting the toolkit around inputs and loops rather than outputs and reports.

Inputs: The Real Competitive Advantage (Data-Backed)

In the modern enterprise, inputs determine outcomes more than media scale. Across automotive and retail environments:

- A 10% improvement in audience quality routinely produces a 20–40% improvement in ROAS
- Loss of persistent identity resets optimization

curves by 3–6 months

- Enterprises relying on third-party audiences alone experience learning decay, not learning lift, in AI systems

Jim understood the non-negotiable truth of the AI era:

AI does not fix bad inputs.

It accelerates their consequences.

That's why Mudd's toolkit prioritized:

- Economic reality (ability to pay)
- Behavioral continuity (past actions)
- Geographic compression (ZIP-level behavior)
- Temporal relevance (when decisions are actually made)

Those inputs produced something rare in enterprise marketing: predictability.

Identity as an Appreciating Asset

Most organizations treat identity data as exhaust.

Jim treated it as capital.

Longitudinal analysis showed:

- Enterprises that retained household-level identity for 36+ months achieved 2–3× faster optimization
- Identity continuity reduced channel experimentation costs by 25–35%
- Persistent identity allowed AI systems to detect cause, not just correlation

Unlike impressions, identity compounds. Every cycle teaches the next one. Every campaign inherits the intelligence of the last. That is why identity ownership isn't an IT concern.

It's a *leadership asset decision.*

Closed-Loop Measurement: From

Attribution to Accountability

Most attribution models answer: *"Where did the click come from?"*

Closed-loop systems answer: *"What decision did this spend actually influence?"*

In enterprise environments using full loop closure (media → CRM/DMS → sales):

- Waste from over-frequency dropped 20–35%
- Cost per sale stabilized even when media prices increased
- Budget confidence replaced budget anxiety

The critical difference wasn't sophistication.

It was discipline.

Every dollar had to come home with a story.

Time as a Hidden Variable (with Benchmarks)

When Mudd began treating time as a first-class input, the results were immediate. Data revealed:

- Appointment show rates peaked on specific days of the month, not randomly
- Buyers exposed to coordinated media 10–14 days before decision windows converted at a higher gross
- AI follow-up within 24–72 hours of peak engagement doubled the response compared to instant or delayed outreach

Time was not urgent.

Time was *aligned.*

When enterprises aligned message, medium, and follow-up to natural decision rhythms, chaos disappeared.

The Economics of Waste Reduction

Jim often reframed performance improvement in one word: *Waste.* Enterprise marketing waste typically comes from:

- Reaching households that cannot buy
- Over-frequency after saturation
- Late intervention
- Reset learning curves

Across Mudd-managed systems:

- Reducing geographic waste alone reclaimed 15–25% of the spend
- Audience refinement improved net margin without increasing volume
- Predictable months replaced “heroic” months

Growth became quieter. More reliable. More scalable.

The Toolkit Is a Transferable Discipline

Jim was clear: This toolkit was not automotive-specific. Hospitals, banks, retailers, and franchises faced the same realities:

- Distributed demand
- Identity fragmentation
- Long decision cycles
- High cost of mistakes

The enterprises that outperformed didn't have better dashboards. They had:

- Better inputs
- Better loops
- Better timing
- Better ownership

Tools came and went. Thinking endured.

Synthesis

The enterprise marketer's new toolkit is not a collection of platforms. It is a *system of discipline* built around:

- Seeing behavior early

- Acting before proximity becomes pain
- Preserving identity across time
- Closing every loop
- Letting technology serve learning—not define it

Jim knew that was the difference between surviving disruption and quietly taking market share while others debated dashboards.

And that, ultimately, is the heart of *The Ad Man 2.0.*

Succession: How the Thinking Outlives Jim

Jim never talked much about succession. Not because he hadn't thought about it—but because he believed most succession plans were built backward.

They focused on:

- Who would take over
- What roles would change
- Which tools would be handed down

Very few focused on what way of thinking would survive pressure.

Jim had watched enough leadership transitions to know the pattern: When a founder leaves, what disappears first isn't effort or talent.

It's *judgment.*

The unspoken instincts.
The sequencing.
The quiet decisions that never made it into process documents.

That's what Jim refused to lose.

Why Systems Were Never the Point

From the outside, it might have looked like Jim was building technology. From the inside, he was doing something else.

He was *encoding judgment.*

Every framework—zip-level thinking, closed-loop measurement, proximity-based prioritization, identity ownership—was a way of making instinct *teachable.*

Jim didn't want the next generation to copy his decisions. He wanted them to understand how decisions were made.

That distinction mattered.

Because tools change.
Markets shift.
Platforms rise and fall.

But judgment—if properly framed—scales.

What Actually Gets Passed Down

Jim eventually realized succession wasn't about handing off control. It was about ensuring three things survived:

1. How Reality Is Defined

    Not impressions.
    Not activity.
    Not noise.

Reality meant:

- Households, not clicks
- Zip-level behavior, not vague regions
- Outcomes, not proxies

If the next leader saw the market differently, everything else would drift.

2. How Decisions Are Sequenced

Severity versus proximity.
Now versus later.
Fixing what's near before debating what's big.
Without that sequencing, innovative teams still panic.

3. What Is Never Outsourced

Identity
Learning
Judgment
The definition of success

Jim knew the moment those were outsourced, leadership would quietly erode—even if performance looked fine on paper.

That was the legacy.

Not software.

Not dashboards.

A way of thinking that could survive without him in the room.

The Real Succession Test

Jim used one test internally, even if he never formalized it:

If Jim disappears tomorrow, will the organization still know how to make decisions?

Not how to operate.
Not how to report.
Not how to comply.
How to *decide.*

If the answer was yes, succession was working.

If the answer was no, technology had become a crutch instead of a steward.

Cross-Industry Translation: This Is Not an Automotive Book

Jim was clear about something readers often missed at first. This book is set in the automotive industry.

It is not about automotive.

The problems Jim solved—fragmentation, delayed feedback, vendor-driven thinking, loss of identity, decision paralysis—exist everywhere scale exists.

What changes by industry is vocabulary.

What doesn't change is structure.

Healthcare

Hospitals don't sell cars.

They sell trust under pressure.

Yet they face the same challenges:

- Disconnected systems
- Identity is split across departments
- Outcomes are measured long after decisions
- Leaders drowning in dashboards

Zip-level thinking becomes service-area behavior.
Closed-loop measurement becomes outcomes by cohort.
Proximity becomes patient impact now vs. later.

Hospitals that adopt this thinking:

- Reduce readmission waste
- Improve staffing allocation
- Catch risk earlier
- Make technology serve care instead of documentation

Retail & Franchising

Retailers don't struggle with reach.

They struggle with relevance and timing.

The same principles apply:

- Households over impressions
- Persistent identity over campaigns
- Time as a decision variable

Franchise groups using this thinking:

- Stop over-discounting
- Reduce promotional fatigue
- Align inventory with behavior
- Let local reality drive central decisions

Zip codes become trade areas.
VINs become SKUs.
Service cadence becomes purchase rhythm.
Same system. Different nouns.

Financial Services

Banks, credit unions, and lenders live or die by trust and

timing. They face:

- Long decision cycles
- Heavy regulation
- Fragmented identity
- High cost of mistakes

Closed-loop thinking becomes:

- Offer → engagement → action → outcome
- Identity as a lifetime asset
- Proximity as risk detection

Leaders stop reacting to lagging indicators and start managing exposure windows.

B2B, SaaS, and Professional Services

In B2B, the stakes are higher and slower—but no less real.

This thinking translates as:

- Accounts instead of households

- Buying committees instead of families
- Usage behavior instead of service visits

The same failures appear:

- Dashboards without decisions
- AI without context
- Automation without humanity

The same cure applies:

- Own identity
- Close the loop
- Act while problems are near
- Let systems carry judgment forward

Why This Thinking Travels

The reason this framework works across industries is simple.

It is not built on:

- Channels
- Platforms
- Tactics
- Trends

It is built on:

- Human behavior
- Time
- Trust
- Memory
- Decision cost

Those don’t change.

The Quiet Invitation to the Reader

Jim never told people to become him. He told them to build their own way of seeing—and then protect it.

That’s the invitation this book leaves behind:

- Define reality clearly
- Encode judgment into systems
- Refuse to outsource identity
- Decide by proximity, not panic
- Let technology serve what you believe

If readers do that, the book doesn't just end. It continues—inside organizations Jim will never visit, solving problems he'll never see, using a way of thinking that no longer depends on him.

That's succession, not of a role, but of a philosophy.

"Reach tells. Frequency sells."

Ad Man Notes – Key Principles:

Lesson 1: Integration Beats Innovation

The future isn't more tools — it's fewer tools working together.

Lesson 2: Identity Outperforms Impressions

Knowing who the customer is matters more than how often you reach them.

Lesson 3: Orchestration Is the New Advantage

Leaders win by coordinating systems, channels, and timing — not chasing trends.

YOUR KEY NOTES

Chapter 9

Keep Your Eye on The Ball with Darryl Strawberry

"I never had trouble hitting. I had trouble living." Darryl Strawberry

Two Chairs, One Question

No stadium. No stage. No spotlight.

Just two chairs in a simple room and the kind of stillness where truth has room to breathe.

On one side sat Jim, the Ad Man—a man of faith who had spent his life helping dealers and leaders recover focus, rebuild systems, and fight for second chances when the numbers said "done."

On the other sat Darryl Strawberry—Rookie of the Year, eight-time All-Star, World Series champion, one of the most feared hitters of his era, and a man who had learned that success can be loud while the soul unravels in silence.

Jim did not come as a fan. He came as a brother in the same family of faith, a fellow son who knew what pressure can do to a leader who forgets where identity really rests.

"Darryl," Jim began, "a lot of people know your stats and your home runs. But that's not the real story we're here to tell."

The Gift Arrives Before the Foundation

Talent showed up early in Darryl's life; foundation did not.

Jim asked, "When did you realize you were different—

that baseball came easier to you than to most?"

"Early," Darryl said. "Real early. I didn't grind for it the way other kids did. I just showed up, and it was there."

That created the first leadership tension:

- Talent feels like a blessing.
- Without discipline and limits, it becomes a liability.

"When things come easy," Darryl explained, "you don't learn what holds you up when talent runs out."

Ad Man 2.0 margin note:

Talent can take you far. Without a foundation, it cannot bring you home.

Success Without Guardrails

Success came fast.

Money. Fame. Headlines. People saying yes when

someone needed to say no.

“It was intoxicating,” Darryl admitted. “But inside, I was empty. I didn’t know who I was without the game.”

Jim had seen the same pattern in business:

- Revenue soaring while culture erodes.
- More impressions, less integrity.
- Bigger platforms, weaker disciplines.

“No guardrails,” Jim said.

“None,” Darryl replied. “And when you don’t have guardrails, you don’t slow down—you go faster.”

Editorial conclusion:

If success outpaces character, pressure will eventually cash the check.

Living Two Lives

Jim asked quietly, “When did you realize something was

wrong?"

"When I started living two lives," Darryl said. "One everyone could see. One I tried to hide."

On the field: production, poise, power.

Off the field: pain, addiction, escape.

"I was performing at the highest level," he said, "but inside I was breaking. Addiction doesn't start because you're weak. It starts because you're hurting—and hiding."

In Ad Man language:

- The public metrics were green.
- The private fundamentals were deep red.

When Consequences Catch Up

"What finally stopped you?" Jim asked.

"Pain," Darryl said. "Loss. Consequences."

He named the cost:

- Lost trust.
- Lost relationships.
- Lost seasons.
- Lost years.
- Lost himself.

"Talent opened doors," he said, "but character is what keeps you in the room.

For any leader:

Talent opens the room. Character decides if you stay.

Consequences stripped away the illusions and left the simple truth: the life was not working.

The Turning Point: Faith Rewrites Identity

Every transformational story hinges on a moment when pretending stops.

Jim asked softly, “Where did faith come in?”

“At the bottom,” Darryl said. “When there was nothing left to hide behind. When the applause was gone, and my excuses stopped working.”

“That’s where God met me,” he continued. “Faith didn’t erase the consequences. It gave me something I never had before—truth about who I really was and grace to change.”

Identity shifted:

- From “the gifted one” to “the loved one.”
- From “the performer” to “the son.”
- From “the brand” to “the man—flawed, forgiven, accountable.”

Ad Man 2.0 principle:

Identity precedes performance.

If who you are depends on what you produce, pressure will eventually break you.

Faith rebuilt what performance had never secured.

New Systems: Honesty, Accountability, Community

"What did faith actually require of you?" Jim asked.

"Honesty," Darryl said. "No more blaming. No more hiding. No more pretending I was in control when I wasn't."

Real change looked like new systems:

- Accountability instead of isolation.
- Slowing down instead of outrunning the truth.
- Truth before image.
- Community over celebrity. Jim knew the business parallel well:

If your system relies on willpower, it will fail under pressure.

Faith did not just comfort Darryl. It installed guardrails.

When He Took His Eye Off the Ball

Jim leaned into the metaphor both men understood.

"Baseball teaches focus," he said. "Lose it for a split second, and the result is immediate. When did you take your eye off the ball—not just in the game, but in life?"

"That's exactly what happened," Darryl said. "I took my eye off the ball."

"In baseball, the ball is simple. See it. Track it. Stay locked in. But when life got loud—fame, money, expectations, pressure—I stopped focusing on what actually mattered."

He kept swinging. He kept winning on paper. But his focus had drifted.

Success whispered, "You're fine."

Drift had already begun—from fundamentals to feelings, from responsibility to escape, from calling to ego.

For leaders, the translation is clear:

- The ball is what truly matters: faith, family, character, mission.
- Focus is where your attention really rests, not what your slide deck says.
- Pressure does not knock you off course; it exposes what you have been watching all along.

Leaders Don't Collapse; They Drift

"People assume pressure causes failure," Jim said.

"Pressure doesn't cause it," Darryl replied. "Pressure exposes it. When your eye is on the wrong thing—status, pleasure, validation—pressure doesn't knock you down. It just speeds up the consequences."

Leaders rarely fall in a single moment.

- Small compromises.
- Missed conversations.

- Deferred confession.
- Quietly abandoned values.

Jim wrote:

Leaders don't usually fail all at once. They drift.

And another line, for his dealers and teams:

Dashboards can be green while fundamentals are red.

Faith Brings the Ball Back Into View

"What brought your focus back?" Jim asked.

"Faith," Darryl said. "Not religion—relationship. Faith forced me to slow down, to look honestly at myself, and to re-center on what mattered most."

"Faith didn't just forgive me," he added. "It refocused me."

The change could be summarized simply:

- Identity no longer tied to performance.

- Discipline rebuilt from humility.
- Accountability embraced instead of avoided.
- Purpose larger than applause.

Jim wrote one line:

Focus precedes freedom.

From Platform to Stewardship

"How do you see your life now?" Jim asked.

"It looks like service," Darryl said. "God didn't waste my story—the good or the bad."

He described traveling across the country—churches, prisons, recovery programs, teams—speaking to people who were carrying more than they let on.

"I tell them the truth," Darryl said. "About the wins. About the losses. About what happens when you take your eye off the ball—and what happens when grace helps you put it back on what matters."

"People think they're disqualified because of their past," he added. "I remind them adversity isn't the end of the story. Sometimes it's where God starts writing the real one."

Jim recognized the pattern—it sounded like the campaigns he had built for years, only now the 'product' was hope.

Brothers Under the Same Grace

As the conversation slowed, Jim was not looking at a celebrity. He was looking at family.

In his agency world, he had spent his career fighting for second chances—for dealers, for teams, for ideas everyone else had written off.

Now he stood with a man doing the same in a different arena, telling men and women who thought they were finished that the story was not over.

Different careers. Same core:

- Men of faith.
- Sons under the same Father.
- Brothers learning, sometimes the hard way, that grace is stronger than drift.

Jim's Ad Man 2.0 Field Notes

On the drive home, Jim turned story into structure.

His notes read:

Lesson 1: Identity Precedes Performance

If who you are depends on what you produce, pressure will eventually break you. Identity grounded in God's love creates leaders who can weather both wins and losses.

Lesson 2: You Can Win While Losing Focus

Scoreboards and dashboards can look great while a leader's focus has quietly shifted from calling to ego, from service to self.

Lesson 3: Proximity Determines the Cost of Failure

Problems are cheapest when they are closest to the moment they start. Drift unaddressed becomes expensive crisis.

Lesson 4: Systems Fail Without Real Accountability

Willpower is not a strategy. Accountability, truth-telling, and community are leadership systems that keep you honest when life gets loud.

Lesson 5: Reinforcement Shapes Destiny

What you reward—personally and organizationally—becomes culture. Before faith, Darryl reinforced performance and escape. After faith, he reinforced honesty, discipline, and service.

Lesson 6: Scars Create Transferable Leadership

People follow leaders who have walked through failure with integrity. Darryl's scars give him authority to speak to those who feel beyond repair. Lesson 7: Faith Reframes Pressure

Faith does not remove pressure. It reframes it—from a threat to a refining fire, from a verdict to a classroom.

At the bottom of the page, Jim wrote:

Faith restores what drift destroys. Jim had built his agency on the belief that people deserved another chance.

Now Darryl carries that same message into a different arena—telling men and women who think they are finished that their story is not over if they are willing to look up and tell the truth.

Leaders rarely fail in a single swing.

They drift—pitch by pitch, decision by decision—until pressure finally shows them how far they have wandered.

When they turn back to what matters most—back to the God who calls them His own—there is still another pitch to see and another swing to take.

Jim knew that.

Darryl knew that.

Two very different stories, carried by the same Redeemer—proof that the grace that found them is the same grace reaching for you.

<u>Recommended Books By Darryl Strawberry:</u>

https://www.simonandschuster.com/books/Another-Life/Darryl-Strawberry/9781637748848

Ad Man Notes – Key Principles:

Lesson 1: Talent Without Focus Is Fragile

Natural ability must be paired with discipline to endure.

Lesson 2: Distraction Is the Silent Killer of Performance

Success erodes when attention drifts from fundamentals.

Lesson 3: Recovery Begins with Ownership

Accountability — not excuses — restores momentum.

YOUR KEY NOTES

MUDD
ADVERTISING

Chapter 10

Leadership Matters with Ken Blanchard

"The key to successful leadership is influence, not authority. Feedback is the breakfast of champions." Ken Blanchard

Jim always enjoyed conversations that didn't feel rushed.

Not meetings.

Not panels.

Not presentations with slides and clocks.

Honest conversations—the kind where ideas had room to breathe. That was why he was looking forward to this one.

Ken Blanchard was in Iowa for a speaking engagement, and Jim had rearranged his entire day to make sure they could sit together without an agenda. No stopwatch. No podium. Just two chairs near a window that looked out over a quiet stretch of trees beginning to turn.

Ken arrived with a warm smile, the kind that instantly disarmed formality. "Jim," he said, extending his hand, "It's good to see you again."

Jim chuckled, "I've been waiting for this conversation longer than you know."

They sat. Coffee appeared. Silence lingered—not awkwardly, but comfortably. Jim finally broke it. "Ken," he said, "I want to start with a confession."

Ken leaned back. "Those are usually the best places to start."

The Books That Stuck

"I've read a lot of business books," Jim said, "Hundreds, probably. But there are only a handful that changed how I behaved when no one was watching."

Ken agreed, "Behavior is the only thing that matters in the end."

"The One Minute Manager was the first," Jim continued, "One Minute Goals. One Minute Praisings. One Minute Reprimands. It taught me something simple I didn't realize I was missing—clarity."

Ken smiled, "Most performance problems are clarity problems."

"That's exactly it!" Jim admitted, "When expectations are vague, people fill in the gaps with fear."

Ken nodded, "And fear is expensive."

"But Raving Fans," Jim continued, pausing, thinking, "That one stayed with me longer than I expected."

Ken's eyes lit up, "Tell me why."

Jim leaned forward, "Because it didn't treat customer service like a department. It treated it like a promise. And promises create accountability."

Ken let a laugh slip through, "That's what most organizations miss. They measure satisfaction, but they never define loyalty."

Satisfied Isn't Safe

Jim asked the question that had been nagging him for years, "Why do so many companies think 'satisfied' customers are enough?"

Ken didn't answer immediately; he let the question linger. "Because 'satisfied' sounds reassuring," he said finally. "It feels like a finish line."

"But it's not," Jim finished.

"No," Ken replied, "It's a warning sign." He turned his coffee cup slowly in his hands. "A satisfied customer," he said, "will leave you the moment it's easier to do so. They're not loyal. They're just unprovoked."

Jim knew that all too well, saying, "That aligns with what we see in market data. When switching costs drop, satisfaction no longer protects you. Trust does."

Ken smiled, "Exactly. Loyalty only exists when leaving feels like a loss."

Jim added, "We've watched brands with high satisfaction scores still lose market share because they never gave customers a reason to stay."

Ken leaned forward, "Satisfaction measures the past. Loyalty predicts the future."

The Vision Question

Jim flipped open his notebook. "You talk about three steps," he said, "Define a vision. Discover what the customer wants. Deliver the vision... plus one percent."

Ken confessed, "Most organizations skip the first step

and rush to execution." "Deliver?" Jim asked.

"Exactly," Ken said, "They start doing things before they decide what they want to be known for."

Jim felt a chuckle brewing, "That sounds familiar."

"If you don't define the vision," Ken said, "your employees will invent one. And improvised visions don't scale."

Jim paused, writing down Ken's words, then spoke, "We've seen that play out. Teams chase metrics without understanding the promise behind them."

Ken agreed, "And metrics without meaning turn people into mechanics."

"So how do leaders define a service vision that doesn't become a slogan?" Jim asked.

"They define it in behavior," Ken said, "Not words. Not posters."

Ken continued, "You don't say 'we care about customers.' You say, 'Here's what we will always do—even when it costs us time, money, or convenience.'"

Jim nodded slowly, "That's when people trust it."

Plus One Percent

"I've always loved the 'plus one percent' idea," Jim said.

Ken laughed, "People think it means doing more."

"But it doesn't," Jim said.

"No," Ken replied, "It means doing slightly better than expected—consistently."

Jim leaned back, connecting the dots in his mind, "That's what systems are for."

Ken smiled at his friend, "Exactly. Data shows consistency beats intensity every time. Small improvements, repeated daily, outperform big initiatives that fade."

Jim tapped his pen, “We see the same thing in marketing performance. Reliable execution compounds. Heroics burn out.”

“Raving fans,” Ken said, “aren’t created by big moments. They’re created by small moments done right—every time.”

Turning Inward: Gung Ho!

“At some point,” Jim said, “I realized customer loyalty and employee engagement are the same problem—just viewed from different sides.”

“That’s not accidental,” Ken admitted, “Disengaged employees can’t create engaged customers.”

“Spirit of the Squirrel. Way of the Beaver. Gift of the Goose,” Jim said.

Ken proclaimed, “Those ideas gave leaders permission to stop managing people like machines.”

“Why do leaders struggle so much with meaning?” Jim asked.

"Because meaning can't be delegated," Ken replied,

"You can't outsource belief."

Jim nodded, "Engagement surveys confirm that. People don't disengage because of workload. They disengage because the work feels disconnected."

Ken added, "Meaning organizes effort. Without it, people conserve energy."

Meaning Before Metrics

"In my world," Jim said, angling his seat, "data is everywhere. Dashboards. KPIs." Ken nodded emphatically, "Metrics are useful—but they're not motivating."

"Exactly," Jim dove in, "Data tells people how they're doing. Meaning tells them why it matters."

Ken felt a smile pull at his lips, saying, "When people don't know why, they optimize for survival."

"And survival never produces excellence," Jim said.

The Way of the Beaver

“Control. Autonomy. Trust,” Jim said, turning the page in his notebook.

“People perform better when they own their work,” Ken replied.

Jim sighed, already knowing the following line, “But leaders equate control with safety.”

Ken smiled with his reply, “Control scales fear. Trust scales capability.”

Jim sat with that, then said, “We’ve seen that in organizations with high autonomy—lower turnover, higher innovation, better decision speed.”

Ken leaned forward, “Because trust reduces friction.”

The Gift of the Goose

“Encouragement,” Jim said, closing his notebook.

“Recognition isn’t fluff,” Ken replied, “It’s

reinforcement."

Jim chuckled, "Data backs that up. Teams that receive regular recognition outperform peers— and stay longer."

"Because people don't leave work," Ken said, "They leave invisibility."

The Whale That Changed the Conversation

"There's one book of yours people don't expect me to bring up," Jim said.

Ken laughed, already knowing the answer, "Whale Done!"

"It might be the most practical leadership book you wrote," Jim confessed.

"That's because it's about behavior," Ken admitted, "Every reinforced behavior gets repeated."

Jim agreed, “And punished behavior gets hidden.”

Ken acknowledged, “Exactly. Reinforce progress, and people grow.”

Why Ken Wrote These Books

“Why parables?” Jim asked.

“Because pressure erases memory,” Ken answered, “Stories survive stress.”

Jim smiled, “That explains why people remember your lessons decades later.”

Jim’s Reflection

As the light shifted, Jim closed his notebook.
“Leadership isn’t about pushing harder,” he said, “It’s about removing friction—so people can do their best work.”

Ken smiled warmly, “That’s how leadership lasts.”

Outside, the air was cool. The best business lessons don’t

age. They deepen. And the leaders who last aren't the loudest.

They're the ones who learn how to listen.

Recommended Books By Ken Blanchard:

Gung Ho!

Raving Fans

Whale Done!

The One Minute Manager

https://www.kenblanchardbooks.com/books/

Ad Man Notes – Key Principles:

Lesson 1: Leadership Is a Daily Choice, Not a Title

Influence comes from behavior, not position.

Lesson 2: Great Leaders Multiply Others

The true measure of leadership is how many leaders you create.

Lesson 3: Feedback Fuels Growth

Leaders who avoid feedback stop learning.

YOUR KEY NOTES

Chapter 11

Managing with Your HEART and Your HEAD with Alan Mulally

"It is nice to be important but more important to be nice."* *Alan Mulally

"Working Together"™ Is Not a Slogan—It's a Discipline.

The room carried a quiet Jim had come to respect. Not the silence of awkwardness—but the stillness that settles in when two people are willing to slow down long enough to tell the truth.

Jim set his notebook on the table but didn't open it right away.

"Alan," he said, "a lot of people talk about leadership systems. Very few can say, 'I lived this when the stakes were existential.' You can. I want to understand what was real—not what sounds good in hindsight."

Alan Mulally met him calmly.

"That's an important distinction," he said. "Because leadership ideas really matter when they're tested under pressure."

Jim nodded. He had learned that truth the hard way.

The Foundation: Love, Service, and Respect

Alan didn't begin with Boeing and Ford. He began with life.

“My parents taught me something long before I understood business,” he said. “They taught me that the purpose of life is to love and be loved - in that order, and to serve the greater good.”

Jim looked up. “That’s not how most leadership stories start.”

Alan smiled gently. “It should be. If you don’t start there, leadership becomes transactional. You manage outcomes, not people. And when pressure comes, people protect themselves instead of the mission.”

Jim nodded slowly. “I’ve seen fractured organizations.”

“Yes,” Alan said. “Because fear is corrosive. Respect is constructive.”

"Growing up," Alan continued, "life was simple."

“We lived with very modest means,” he said. “Even so, I was incredibly fortunate—because my parents loved me and believed that I could make a significant difference and contribution to our world.”

Jim could hear the gratitude in his voice. Not nostalgia—conviction.

“To that end,” Alan said, “they taught me lessons I’ve carried with me throughout my life.”

He paused, then shared them—quietly and deliberately.

- **The purpose of life is to love and be loved—in that order**
- **To serve is to live**
- **Seek to understand before seeking to be understood**
- **By working together with others, you can make the most positive contribution to the most people**
- **Expect the unexpected and expect to deal with it ... positively**
- **Lifelong learning and continuous improvement**
- **Respect everyone, we are all creatures of God and worthy to be loved**
- **Develop one integrated life that is your life’s work of service**
- **It's nice to be important, but it's more important to be nice**

Jim realized these weren't lessons meant for childhood alone.

They were principles meant to be lived.

This wasn't leadership theory added later.

This was the foundation.

Alan said that all of these convictions that deepened as he grew.

Then he smiled, almost sheepishly.

"And like all kids," he said, "I wanted to fit in."

He wanted a pair of Levi jeans.

Some Weejuns penny loafers.

A car someday.

College, if possible.

"So with my parents' teachings and encouragement," Alan said, "I decided my way forward was to serve. And maybe—if I worked hard—I could earn those special jeans."

Jim smiled. He knew where this was going.

Alan began with *TV Guide* and newspaper routes. Then a lawn-mowing business. He was a bagger, then a checker, then a night manager at the Dillons grocery store. He worked as a carpenter, a ranch hand, and a farm hand. He played sports. In college, he became a fraternity rush chairman and later president.

"All the while," Alan said, "I was learning aerospace engineering—through summer jobs at Beechcraft, Cessna, Boeing, and the University of Kansas."

Jim realized these weren't résumé lines.

They were formation.

"Starting with my very first work," Alan continued, "I became aware of the power and advantage of working together with everyone connected to my service."

He named them easily—because he had lived it.

Customers.
Parents.

Family.

Employers.

Employees.

Suppliers.

Governments.

Communities.

Competitors.

Bankers.

Investors.

"I looked at all work as service," Alan said. "And I loved "Working Together"™ to serve humanity with love and humility to create value and growth for all."

He loved asking customers what they wanted and valued.

He loved the appreciative smiles when they were well served.

He loved learning, growing, and exceeding expectations.

And he loved the deep satisfaction that came from contributing meaningfully to people's lives.

“I loved working together with all the stakeholders to create value for everyone,” Alan said.

“And through every job,” Jim realized, “you were refining something.”

Alan nodded. “Yes. I kept improving my “Working Together”™ principles and practices—through the work culture itself.”

As the scope of his service grew—first at **Boeing** and later at **Ford Motor Company**—Alan continued to develop and refine a clear, disciplined way to live out those beliefs.

This became his Our **"Working Together"™ Leadership and Management System**, which is the practical way to implement principles and practices to work together across complex product programs, global businesses, and diverse stakeholders.

At its core, the system was simple—but never easy.

"Working Together"™ was built on the following

principles and practices:

- **People First . . . Love 'em up**
- **Everyone is included**
- **A Compelling Vision, a Comprehensive Strategy, and Relentless Implementation**
- **Clear performance goals**
- **One plan**
- **Facts and data—because we can't manage a secret, and the data sets us free**
- **Expect the unexpected and expect to deal with it**
- **Everyone knows the plan, the status, and the areas that need special attention**
- **Propose a plan with a positive, "find-a-way" attitude**
- **Respect, listen, help, and appreciate each other**
- **Authentic and emotional resilience—trust the process, and each other**
- **Have fun. Enjoy the journey and each other—never at another's expense**

"*Working Together*"™ Alan said, "proved to be a very reliable process—with clear operating processes and expected behaviors—to manage our organizations including all of our stakeholders."

"It allowed us to sustainably deliver value for the greater good, even as the world around us continued to change rapidly."

Jim could see it clearly now.

This wasn't leadership by personality.

It was leadership by principle, practice, and process—grounded in respect for people and disciplined execution over time.

Boeing: Alignment Before Scale

"What did Boeing teach you," Jim asked, "that prepared you for Ford?"

Alan's voice was steady.

"Boeing taught me alignment at scale. When people understand the mission—connecting the world safely and efficiently—they will work through enormous complexity together."

"But alignment doesn't happen by accident," he added. "It requires clarity, communication, and constant implementation."

Jim smiled. "That sounds like the early form of "Working Together™."

"It was," Alan said.

Where "Working Together"™ Was Forged

Alan spent thirty-seven years at Boeing, working through demanding seasons where precision mattered and consequences were real. Under his leadership, Boeing became the most successful commercial airplane company in the world.

At Boeing, "*Working Together*"™ became a leadership and management system—grounded in love, respect, discipline, and service to humanity.

Boeing didn't just produce airplanes.

It produced leaders who understood that systems exist to serve people—and that people, when respected, create extraordinary value.

Alan Mulally: The Leader Behind the System

As Jim listened, he realized something else needed to be said plainly—not to impress, but to establish truth.

Alan Mulally's leadership was not situational.

It was lived, tested, and sustained over decades.

Alan served as President and Chief Executive Officer of Ford Motor Company and as a member of Ford's Board of Directors from 2006 to 2014. During that time, he led Ford's transformation into one of the world's leading automobile companies and the number one automotive brand in the United States.

Before Ford, Alan served nearly four decades at Boeing,

rising to become Executive Vice President of The Boeing Company, President and CEO of Boeing Commercial

Airplanes, and President of Boeing Information, Space & Defense Systems.

Throughout his career, Alan developed and lived an authentic, committed, connected, collaborative, and aligned culture—love by design to create value and growth for all stakeholders and the greater good.

Jim closed his notebook for a moment.

This was not accidental leadership.

This was a life spent building systems that help people succeed—working together.

Why Alan Chose Ford

When the conversation turned to Ford, Jim noticed something unmistakable.

There was no hesitation in Alan's voice.

"I believed in the Ford team," Alan said. "Their capability. Their pride. Their desire to win the right way."

"And I believed in the dealers," he added. "They're entrepreneurs. They live the brand in their communities. When the company and the dealers work from the same vision and the same facts, extraordinary things happen."

This decision wasn't driven by ego.

It was driven by values and beliefs.

The Ford Moment: Truth or Collapse

"When I arrived at Ford," Alan said, "the company was losing billions of dollars. But the losses weren't the root problem."

"The real issue was fragmentation," he continued.

"Regions and business units operated independently."

“No shared various situational information,” Jim said.

“Exactly,” Alan replied. “And without it, you cannot work together.”

The Business Plan Review: “Working Together”™ Made Visible

“We needed one plan,” Alan said. “One team. One set of facts. Every week.”

The Business Plan Review wasn’t about control.

It was about serving the organization by making reality visible to all.

Green meant on plan.

Yellow meant issue.
Red meant help needed with the issue.
“Red was never failure,” Alan said. “Red was leadership and so appreciated.”

What "Working Together"™ Accomplished at Ford

Before the financial crisis fully unfolded, Alan made one of the most decisive moves of his career. In 2006, he

secured **$23.6 billion** in financing, mortgaging nearly all of Ford's assets. The move was questioned at the time. History would later call it foresight.

That capital allowed Ford to navigate the Great Recession **without a government bailout**—preserving independence, pride, and trust.

One Ford

Alan introduced **One Ford**—not as a slogan, but as a unifying global strategy.

One team.

One plan.

One shared direction.

Ford streamlined its product portfolio, reduced platforms, divested non-core brands, and refocused on high-quality, fuel-efficient vehicles customers could trust.

This wasn't cost-cutting for optics.

It was clarity reducing complexity.

Culture, Accountability, and Results

The Business Plan Review made accountability safe.

Problems surfaced early.

Trust deepened.

Decisions accelerated.

Employee engagement rose.

Silos weakened.

Pride and encouragement returned.

By 2009, Ford returned to profitability.

By 2012, Ford's bonds regained value.

Ford emerged as the only major U.S. automaker to avoid

a government bailout.

This wasn't just a financial recovery.

It was a brand service recovery.

Bill Ford's Belief Made the System Possible

Alan didn't do this alone.

Bill Ford believed in Alan—and in "Working Together"™.

That belief was active and unwavering.

Bill aligned the Board, reinforced the Compelling Vision, supported the comprehensive strategy, and protected the relentless positive implementation plan.

Trust at the top became courage throughout the organization.

Two Great Companies. One Shared Belief.

Jim was careful not to frame this as one company saving another.

That wasn't the truth.

Boeing and Ford were already great companies.

What connected them was values.

Boeing forged the system.

Ford had the wisdom and the talent to adopt it.

Alan had the integrity to lead it and love it.

And the Ford team—and its dealers—lived it successfully "WorkingTogether"™.

The Legacy That Endures

Henry Ford built a company on the belief that industry could serve humanity.

Decades later, that belief stood renewed.

History will remember what Alan Mulally and Bill Ford did together—not simply as a turnaround, but as a return to greatness grounded in values and successful working together leadership and culture.

As Jim reflected, the deeper pattern became unmistakable.

Alan's authentic leadership aligns everyone in how to be and how to do to serve.

Everything else followed.

Jim believed Henry Ford would be proud.

Two great companies.
One way of leading.
People—respected, aligned, and trusted—doing their very best work together.

ALAN'S LEADERSHIP AND SERVICE BIO

Alan Mulally served as president and chief executive officer of the Ford Motor Company and as a member of Ford's board of directors from 2006 - 2014. Mulally led Ford's transformation into one of the world's leading automobile companies and the #1 automobile brand in the United States. He guided Ford in working together on a compelling vision, comprehensive strategy, and implementation of the One Ford plan to deliver profitable growth for all of the company's stakeholders.

Prior to joining Ford, Mulally served as executive vice president of the Boeing Company, president and CEO of Boeing Commercial Airplanes, and president of Boeing Information, Space and Defense Systems from 1969 – 2006 where he created his "Working Together" Leadership and Management System for global aerospace leadership.

Throughout his career, Mulally has developed and nurtured his Our "Working Together" Leadership and Management System and Our Connected, Collaborative, and Aligned Culture of Love by

Design to Create Value and Growth for All the Stakeholders and the Greater Good. Mulally has been recognized for his contributions, industry leadership, and service, including being named #3 on *Fortune's* "World's Greatest Leaders," one of the 30 "World's Best CEO's" by *Barrons'* magazine, one of "The World's Most influential People" by *Time* magazine, "Chief Executive of the Year" by *Chief Executive* magazine, Engineer of the Year by *Design News*, and the Leader of the Future by the Frances Hesselbein Leadership Institute in 2006. He was also honored with the American Society for Quality's medal for excellence in executive leadership, the Automotive Executive of the Year, and the Thomas Edison Achievement Award. Mulally is a Museum of Flight Pathfinder and a member of the Automobile Hall of Fame. Most recently, Alan was recognized with the USA Baldrige Foundation's 2025 Lifetime Leadership Service Award.

Mulally previously served on President Obama's United States Export Council. He served as co-chairman of the Washington Competitiveness Council and has served on the advisory boards of the National Aeronautics and Space Administration, the University of Washington, the University of Kansas, the Massachusetts Institute of Technology, the United States Air Force Scientific Advisory Board, and United States Business Roundtable. Mulally has also served as President of the American Institute of Aeronautics and Astronautics and as Chairman of the Board of Governors of the Aerospace Industries Association. Mulally is a member of the United

States National Academy of Engineering and a fellow of England's Royal Academy of Engineering.

Mulally currently serves on the board of directors of Google, Carbon 3D, and the Mayo Clinic. Mulally holds Bachelor and Master of Science degrees in Aeronautical and Astronautical Engineering from the University of Kansas, and a Masters in Management from the Massachusetts Institute of Technology as an Alfred P. Sloan Fellow

For more details check out this QR CODE Link Online

ALAN'S "WORKING TOGETHER"™ © KEY REFERNCES

- "A Conversation with Alan Mulally about His "Working Together"© Strategic, Operational, and Stakeholder-Centered Management System," Alan Mulally and Sarah McArthur, *Leader to Leader,* Volume 2022, Issue 104. PDF.

- *Work Is Love Made Visible: A Collection of Essays About the Power of Finding Your Purpose from the World's Greatest Thought Leaders*, Frances Hesselbein, Marshall Goldsmith, Sarah McArthur, foreword Alan Mulally. Amazon."People

- "Working Together"© to Produce the Preferred Boeing 777 Airplane Family," Sarah McArthur, Alan Mulally, Dan Dornseif, Michael Lombardi, Peter M. Morton, Lars Andersen, Ron Ostrowski, and John Roundhill, *Leader to Leader, Volume 2025, Issue 117*, Wiley, May 19, 2025. PDF.

- *American Icon: Alan Mulally and the Fight to Save Ford Motor Company*, Bryce Hoffman.

- "Engineer of the Year Alan Mulally" Lawrence D. Maloney, *Design News*, March 4, 1996.

- USA Baldrige Foundation's 2025 Lifetime Leadership Service Award "Announcing Recipients of Baldrige Foundation Leadership Awards for 2025," *Baldrige Foundation*, January 28, 2025. Instagram Post and X Post. 2025 E. David Spong Lifetime Achievement Award: Alan Mulally, *Baldrige Foundation*, April 1, 2025. A Conversation with Alan Mulally, *Baldrige Foundation*, April 1, 2025. "Leading with Love and Excellence: How "Working Together" © Implements the Baldrige Excellence Framework," Debbie Collard, Susan Ireland, and Sarah McArthur, *Leader to Leader, Volume 2025, Issue 118*, Wiley, August 11, 2025.

- *The Extraordinary Power of Leader Humility: Thriving Organizations - Great Results,* foreword and chapter by Alan Mulally about how leader humility enables and nurtures effective working together by great teams, Marilyn Gist, PhD. Amazon.

- "Drive One Direction: How To Unleash The Accelerating Power of Alignment and Jesus' Thoughts," **Dave Ramos, September 23, 2024.**

Ad Man Notes – Key Principles:

Lesson 1: Compassion and Discipline Are Not Opposites

The strongest cultures balance empathy with accountability.

Lesson 2: Transparency Builds Trust

Truth shared early prevents fear later.

Lesson 3: Alignment Beats Control

When people understand the mission, micromanagement disappears.

YOUR KEY NOTES

Chapter 12

No One Does This Alone

"There is a destiny that makes us all brothers, no one goes on his way alone. All that we give into the lives of others comes back into our own." Edwin Markham

If you are still reading, you already know something most people never learn: there are no shortcuts that last. Real success is slow, steady, and on purpose. And it is also hard.

Every idea in this book was paid for—over time, through mistakes, long nights, missed sleep, and sometimes tears. I did not think my way into these principles. I lived my way into them, often the hard way.

That distinction matters.

Because anyone can repeat ideas they've heard. Only experience teaches you which ones hold up under pressure.

What I Know for Sure

Here is what has proven true, no matter the season.

You have to face the facts—about the numbers, the market, and yourself. Wishing never fixed a balance sheet, never saved a company, and never strengthened a family.

You control your attitude, your effort, your preparation, and your promises. That is enough responsibility to keep you busy for a lifetime.

People and culture beat brilliance over time. Clear goals, absolute ownership, and honest encouragement will always outperform clever slogans and shiny strategies.

Prosperity is a test, not a trophy. When God blesses you, the real question is not how much you accumulate, but whether others are better off because you were here.

Those truths turned a basement and a garage-sale desk into an agency on a twenty-acre campus. But the buildings were never the point. The client list was never the point.

The point was what it took to get there—and who walked the road with me.

What It Really Costs

Nothing about this story was easy.

KCFI failed. And I had to go home and explain that—to Cecelia, my wife for 54 years, and to our kids. Then we had to decide whether we dared to start again.

In 1981, we opened an agency in the basement during a recession. Some days, the phone never rang. Some weeks, payroll looked bigger than our faith. There were nights I lay awake staring at the ceiling, wondering if I had made a mistake I could not undo.

Along the way, I misjudged people. I made hasty calls. I spoke when I should have listened. We lived through downturns, client losses, health scares, and the funerals of friends.

None of it was neat.
None of it was scripted.
And none of it was painless.

If anything in these pages has sounded too smooth, let me say this clearly: it wasn't. The road was rough, and I bear the marks.

And yet, I would not trade it—because of the people God put beside me.

The Decision That Mattered Most

If you remember only one thing from this book, remember this:

No one does life—or leadership—alone. Choose your partner wisely.

I did not live this story by myself.

God gave me a voice and a stubborn will. Then, *He* gave me Cecelia.

She kept the books.
She raised the children.
She steadied the ship while I was out selling, broadcasting, and building.

The agency may have carried my name, but it ran on our life together.

When KCFI went under, she did not blame. She stood with me. When a friend said, "Mudd, you ought to start your own agency," she went with Mary Kay and bought that first desk at a garage sale. We started over side by side.

We did not avoid storms.
We faced them together.

We prayed. We argued. We forgave. And then we went back to work.

Over the years, that single choice—to walk together—shaped everything: how we did business, how we treated people, how we gave, and how we measured success.

Here is the plain truth from a man who had his name on the sign: Whatever good people credit to me, they should also credit to her.

So, I will repeat it, as plainly as I know how:

The most crucial leadership decision you will ever make is who you choose to join your life with.

That is true in marriage first. It is also true in business, friendships, and the mentors you allow close to you.

Ask yourself:

· Do they share my deepest convictions?

· Will they tell me the truth?

· Will they stand and pray with me when it all goes wrong?

If not, think twice before you hand them the wheel.

What We Tried to Leave

We began in Owensboro and Monmouth and somehow found ourselves woven into the Cedar Valley and far beyond. We never set out to become a "story." We set out to be faithful where we were.

What remains now is simple.

A company built on Family, Teamwork, and Excellence, still saying, "We love it when you succeed," and meaning it.

A community with stronger churches, schools, and charities because people chose to give back what they had been given.

A family that understands thoughts have consequences, that negativity is a road to nowhere, and that the best measure of a life is how many others are standing because you showed up.

The Road Ahead

The tools and stories in this book are now yours.

Use them.

Improve them.

Pass them on.

But do not forget the heart of it.

Set your true north.

Walk the long road on purpose.

And remember that no one does life alone—and no one should want to.

Choose your partner wisely.

I chose Cecelia.

The rest is history.

— *The Ad Man*

"You can't expect to win if you don't show up every day."

<u>Ad Man Notes – Key Principles</u>:

Lesson 1: Success Is Always a Team Outcome

Solo leadership is a myth; results are collective.

Lesson 2: Gratitude Strengthens Culture

Recognition reinforces belonging and loyalty.

Lesson 3: Legacy Is Shared, Not Owned

What lasts is built together.

<u>YOUR KEY NOTES</u>

Thank you!

Chapter 13

The People Who Made It Possible

"When we focus on our gratitude, the tide of disappointment goes out, and the tide of love rushes in." Kirstin Armstrong

Before I go any further, there is something I need to say out loud.

Over the last forty years, *thousands of people* have carried the weight of this work with me. Not in theory—in practice. They showed up early, stayed late, cared deeply, and did the complex, often unseen work that no founder ever does alone.

To every member of the Mudd team—past and present—please know this: Your contribution was irreplaceable. You were not an interchangeable part in a growing firm.

You were craftsmen, problem-solvers, mentors, encouragers, and truth-tellers. You carried clients when they were struggling. You challenged ideas when they needed sharpening. You protected the culture when shortcuts would have been easier.

This firm did not succeed because of one person's vision. It succeeded because of shared commitment, shared responsibility, and shared belief—day after day, year after year.

I also want to thank our dealer partners, who trusted us not just with advertising, but with their livelihoods. You treated us as partners, not vendors. You challenged us, supported us, and stayed committed to continuous improvement—especially when the work demanded change instead of comfort.

Your loyalty and trust shaped our thinking as much as any internal strategy ever did.

And to the OEM partners who stood with us over the years—thank you for believing that things could keep improving. You supported innovation before outcomes were guaranteed. You encouraged progress when it required patience. You trusted that people, processes, and ideas could get better if we stayed honest and committed.

To every employee, every partner, every dealer, every automotive relationship—please hear this clearly: *I carry deep gratitude and genuine love for you.*

If anything good came from these forty-five years, it came because you chose to walk the road with us.

Those Who Supported the Work from the Outside

There is another group whose contribution must be named—because without them, none of this would have been possible.

To the Mudd family members, thank you for the sacrifices that never showed up on an org chart. You shared time that could not be replaced. You carried uncertainty quietly. You supported long days, hard seasons, and decisions that asked more than they gave back in the moment.

This work demanded patience, grace, and belief—not just from those inside the firm, but from those who stood behind it.

And to the families of our employees, I want to say this clearly: Your support meant more to us than you may ever know.

You encouraged loved ones to keep learning, to keep improving, to stay committed to doing the work the right way. You believed in the Mudd team—sometimes before outcomes were clear— and you carried the unseen weight that allowed others to show up fully.

Culture does not live only at work. It lives at dinner tables, in late conversations, and in the quiet encouragement to try again tomorrow.

For that belief, that patience, and that shared commitment to improvement—I am deeply grateful.

To our Mudd Family of clients . . . There are SO MANY of you that have helped over the years,

Too many to possibly print . . . We'd like to share our special thanks:

Jim Mudd, Clifton Lambreth, Rob Mudd & The Entire Mudd Family

Ad Man Notes – Key Principles:

Lesson 1: People Are the Strategy

Systems fail without committed humans behind them.

Lesson 2: Loyalty Is Earned Through Respect

Longevity comes from mutual trust.

Lesson 3: Culture Is Remembered Longer Than Campaigns

How people are treated outlives any tactic.

YOUR KEY NOTES

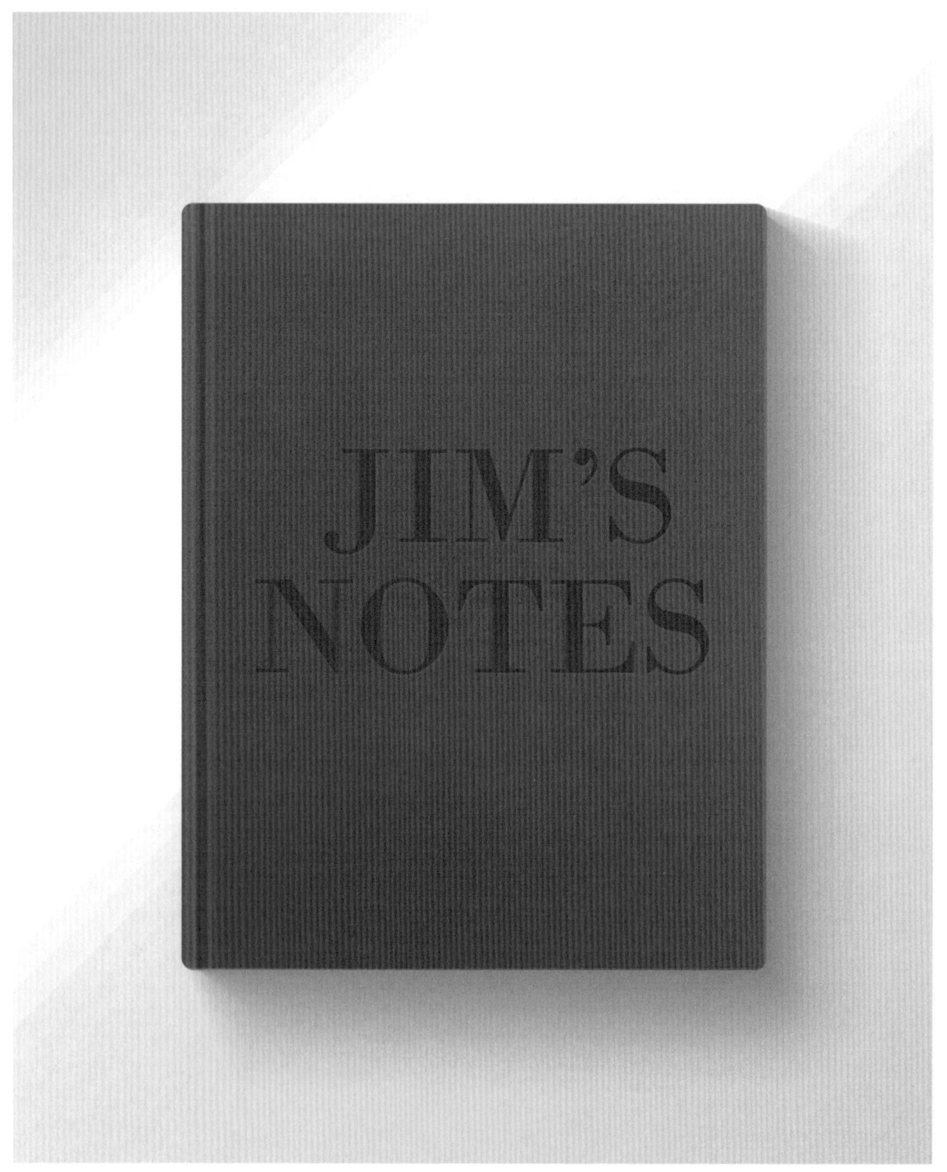
JIM'S
NOTES

Chapter 14

True North Principles
Jim’s Little Black Book

PEOPLE

How leaders treat others, build trust, and grow human potential

· “The best leaders create a vision, articulate the vision, passionately own the vision, and relentlessly drive it to completion.” — Jack Welch

· “People may hear your words, but they feel your attitude.” — John C. Maxwell

· “A leader is one who knows the way, goes the way, and shows the way.” — John C. Maxwell

· “Leadership is not about being in charge. It is about taking care of those in your charge.” — Simon Sinek

· “The greatest leaders are those who empower others to become leaders.” — Unknown

· “Kindness is the language which the deaf can hear and the blind can see.” — Mark Twain

· “The single biggest problem in communication is the illusion that it has taken place.” — George Bernard Shaw

· “Treat people as if they were what they ought to be, and you help them become what they are capable of being.” — Johann Wolfgang von Goethe

Leadership takeaway:

People don’t rise to expectations—they rise to belief, clarity, and respect.

SUCCESS

Resilience, endurance, and the long road of meaningful achievement

· "Success usually comes to those who are too busy to be looking for it." — Henry David Thoreau

· "Don't be distracted by criticism. Remember—the only taste of success some people get is to take a bite out of you." — Zig Ziglar

· "Success is walking from failure to failure with no loss of enthusiasm." — Winston Churchill

· "The difference between who you are and who you want to be is what you do." — Unknown

· "Small disciplines repeated with consistency every day lead to great achievements over time." — John C. Maxwell

· "Perseverance is not a long race; it is many short races one after the other." — Walter Elliot

· "Fall seven times, stand up eight." — Japanese proverb

· “Energy and persistence conquer all things.” — Benjamin Franklin

Leadership takeaway:

Success compounds quietly long before it ever shows up loudly.

PROCESSES

Execution, discipline, and turning intention into results

· “Without continual growth and progress, such words as improvement, achievement, and success have no meaning.” — Benjamin Franklin

· “Excellence is not an act, but a habit.” — Aristotle

· “Plans are nothing; planning is everything.” — Dwight D. Eisenhower

· “If you don’t design your own life plan, chances are you’ll fall into someone else’s.” — Jim Rohn

· “You cannot improve what you do not measure.” — Peter Drucker

· “Success is where preparation and opportunity meet.” — Bobby Unser

· “Well done is better than well said.” — Benjamin Franklin

· “The strength of the team is each individual member. The strength of each member is the team.” — Phil Jackson

Leadership takeaway:

Good intentions don’t execute themselves—process does.

PRINCIPLES

Values, beliefs, and how leaders decide when it matters most

· “In matters of conscience, the law of the majority has no place.” — Mahatma Gandhi

· “If you don’t stand for something, you will fall for anything.” — Malcolm X

· “Character is doing the right thing when nobody’s looking.” — J.C. Watts

· “The time is always right to do what is right.” — Martin Luther King Jr.

· “Live as if you were to die tomorrow. Learn as if you were to live forever.” — Mahatma Gandhi

· “Our lives begin to end the day we become silent about things that matter.” — Martin Luther King Jr.

· “He who has a why to live can bear almost any how.” — Friedrich Nietzsche

· “Values are like fingerprints. Nobody’s are the same, but you leave them all over everything you do.” — Elvis Presley

Leadership takeaway:

Principles are what leaders lean on when pressure removes convenience.

Top 20 Scriptures for Leadership, Life, and Endurance

These are not verses for display. They are verses for decision-making—when pressure is real and clarity matters.

PEOPLE & SERVICE

How leaders treat others

1. Mark 10:45

"For even the Son of Man did not come to be served, but to serve..."

Why it matters: Leadership is responsibility, not privilege.

2. Philippians 2:3–4

"Do nothing out of selfish ambition or vain conceit..."

Why it matters: Humility scales trust.

3. Colossians 3:23

"Whatever you do, work at it with all your heart..."

Why it matters: Excellence honors people and purpose.

4. Romans 12:10

“Be devoted to one another in love...”

Why it matters: Culture is built through daily respect.

5. Proverbs 27:17

“As iron sharpens iron, so one person sharpens another.”

Why it matters: Accountability done well strengthens both sides.

TRUTH, WISDOM & CLARITY

How leaders decide

6. Proverbs 3:5–6

“Trust in the Lord with all your heart...”

Why it matters: Wisdom begins where control ends.

7. John 8:32

"Then you will know the truth, and the truth will set you free."

Why it matters: Truth enables alignment.

8. James 1:5

"If any of you lacks wisdom, you should ask God..."

Why it matters: Leaders are learners first.

9. Proverbs 16:9

"In their hearts humans plan their course..."

Why it matters: Planning matters—but humility matters more.

10. Psalm 119:105

"Your word is a lamp for my feet..."

Why it matters: Clarity comes one step at a time.

DISCIPLINE, PROCESS & STEWARDSHIP

How work gets done faithfully

11. Luke 16:10

“Whoever can be trusted with very little can also be trusted with much.”

Why it matters: Small disciplines predict big responsibility.

1. Proverbs 21:5

“The plans of the diligent lead to profit...”

Why it matters: Discipline outperforms impulse.

2. 1 Corinthians 14:40

“But everything should be done in a fitting and orderly way.”

Why it matters: Order creates trust.

3. Ecclesiastes 7:12

“Wisdom preserves those who have it.”

Why it matters: Wisdom compounds over time.

4. Matthew 25:21

Well done, good and faithful servant..."

Why it matters: Faithfulness precedes reward.

Scriptures for Leadership, Life, and Endurance

They are verses for decision-making—when pressure is real and clarity matters.

PEOPLE & SERVICE

How leaders treat others

1. Mark 10:45

"For even the Son of Man did not come to be served, but to serve..."

Why it matters: Leadership is responsibility, not privilege.

2. Philippians 2:3–4

"Do nothing out of selfish ambition or vain conceit..."

Why it matters: Humility scales trust.

3. Colossians 3:23

"Whatever you do, work at it with all your heart..."

Why it matters: Excellence honors people and purpose.

4. Romans 12:10

"Be devoted to one another in love..."

Why it matters: Culture is built through daily respect.

5. Proverbs 27:17

"As iron sharpens iron, so one person sharpens another."

Why it matters: Accountability done well strengthens both sides.

TRUTH, WISDOM & CLARITY

How leaders decide

6. Proverbs 3:5–6

"Trust in the Lord with all your heart..."

Why it matters: Wisdom begins where control ends.

7. John 8:32

"Then you will know the truth, and the truth will set you free."

Why it matters: Truth enables alignment.

8. James 1:5

"If any of you lacks wisdom, you should ask God..."

Why it matters: Leaders are learners first.

9. Proverbs 16:9

"In their hearts humans plan their course..."

Why it matters: Planning matters—but humility matters more.

10. Psalm 119:105

"Your word is a lamp for my feet..."

Why it matters: Clarity comes one step at a time.

DISCIPLINE, PROCESS & STEWARDSHIP

How work gets done faithfully

11. Luke 16:10

"Whoever can be trusted with very little can also be trusted with much."

Why it matters: Small disciplines predict big responsibility.

12. Proverbs 21:5

"The plans of the diligent lead to profit..."

Why it matters: Discipline outperforms impulse.

13. 1 Corinthians 14:40

"But everything should be done in a fitting and orderly way."

Why it matters: Order creates trust.

14. Ecclesiastes 7:12

"Wisdom preserves those who have it."

Why it matters: Wisdom compounds over time.

15. Matthew 25:21

“Well done, good and faithful servant...”

Why it matters: Faithfulness precedes reward.

PERSEVERANCE, FAITH & ENDURANCE

How leaders endure pressure

16. Galatians 6:9

“Let us not become weary in doing good...”

Why it matters: Consistency wins quietly.

17. Isaiah 40:31

“Those who hope in the Lord will renew their strength.”

Why it matters: Renewal fuels longevity.

18. Romans 8:28

“In all things God works for the good...”

Why it matters: Perspective steadies leadership.

19. Joshua 1:9

“Be strong and courageous...”

Why it matters: Courage is a daily decision.

20. Micah 6:8

“Act justly, love mercy, and walk humbly with your God.”

Why it matters: This is the leadership test that never changes.

Ad Man Notes – Key Principles:

Lesson 1: Principles Outlast Playbooks

When markets change, values remain the compass.

Lesson 2: Consistency Builds Credibility

Doing the right thing repeatedly earns trust.

Lesson 3: Leadership Is Stewardship

The role of a leader is to protect what matters while preparing for what's next.

<u>YOUR KEY NOTES</u>

Appendix

For more details check out this QR CODE Link Online

BIO'S

Jim Mudd Sr.

Jim Mudd Sr. was the founder and chief spiritual officer of Mudd Advertising, headquartered in Cedar Falls, Iowa, and became a trusted ally and innovator for thousands of automotive dealers nationwide. As chairman of the board, he helped shape the company's vision and strategy, guiding it from a basement startup into one of the nation's largest privately held agencies focused exclusively on retail automotive advertising. From the beginning, Jim pushed dealers toward data-driven, results-based campaigns—using a "scientific approach" to media and messaging long before analytics became standard in the industry.

Jim launched Mudd Advertising in 1981 with a single local auto dealer and a simple goal: build campaigns that measurably move metal. Under his leadership, Mudd became an early adopter of integrated traditional and digital strategies—combining direct mail, TV and radio, targeted video, email, and emerging digital channels into coordinated campaigns that helped dealers reach in market buyers more efficiently. He also invested heavily in in house capabilities, adding a state-of-the-art production studio in 2007 and a creative loft in 2010 so dealers could access broadcast-quality video and creative work under one roof—unusual for a regional automotive agency at the time.

Across four decades, Jim helped shape best practices for automotive marketing by insisting on clear offers, consistent branding, and measurable ROI in every campaign. He shared these principles with more than 250 dealer and industry audiences and codified them in The Ad Man, a book he intended as a roadmap and tribute to the auto dealer that outlines a repeatable blueprint for retail success.

Jim graduated from Brescia University in Owensboro, Kentucky, and studied radio and television broadcasting at Northwestern University in Evanston, Illinois, bringing a broadcaster's sense of storytelling and timing into dealership advertising. After a respected career in broadcasting and radio station ownership in the Midwest, he followed the encouragement of dealer partners to create an automotive advertising agency in July 1981—a move that helped modernize how many dealers approached media, messaging, and customer follow up. He served on the national board of the Lead Like Jesus ministry, on the University of Northern Iowa Foundation board, and supported numerous charitable organizations as a generous philanthropist. Jim and his wife and business partner, Cecelia, have both passed away and are remembered as pioneers whose family and team continue their mission of serving the automotive industry with

data driven creativity, servant leadership, and unwavering commitment to dealer success.

Clifton Peter Lambreth

Clifton Peter Lambreth is a highly sought-after business, marketing and automotive industry specialist, published author and television personality. Speaking to numerous organizations, he frequently tours the nation to present on success and business principles and has authored numerous articles on diversity, leadership, compensation and other business topics.

For over 26 years, Clifton proudly served the Ford Motor Company in a variety of positions. He was consistently a top performer throughout his career at Ford and received many prestigious awards and distinctions including five Ford Inuksuk Drive for Leaders Award, three Diversity Leadership awards and the 2008 Ford Leadership Award. Clifton has been a Ford college recruiter for over ten years at Cornell University, University of Pennsylvania, Johnson Business School

and Wharton Business School. He graduated from Thomasville Senior High School in North Carolina having been a proud alumnus of the North Carolina Baptist Children's Mills Home. He went on to receive his BSBA in Marketing and Management and his MBA from Western Carolina University.
Further, he is the founder and CEO of Daniel Bradley Matthews, Inc., a firm that provides strategic automotive, business and marketing consulting.

Due to his expertise and experience, Clifton has been quoted in over 400 media sources. He has done over 150 live radio show interviews and has appeared on NBC, CBS, ABC and Fox TV discussing a multitude of business topics. His first book, *Ford and the American Dream: Founded on Right Decisions*, has been translated into Russian.

Clifton has served on the Board of Directors of the Family Foundation Fun; on the Executive Advisory Board of Lead like Jesus Foundation; Western Carolina's Alumni Board; and on the Advisory Board for Western

Carolina University's School of Business; and he is serving on the board of Directors and Good Seeds Board of Directors and on the University of Tennessee Advisory Board for the Customer Experience Program. Clifton resides in Brentwood, Tennessee.

Rob Mudd

Robert Mudd is a Chief Futurist and global automotive marketing pioneer and innovator, recognized internationally for pioneering data-driven, outcome-focused advertising solutions that help dealers win in the "new now" of automotive retail. With more than three decades of experience spanning North America, Europe, Asia, and Russia, he blends deep industry expertise, digital innovation, and compelling storytelling to drive measurable growth for clients worldwide.

PROFESSIONAL OVERVIEW

- Chief Futurist at Mudd Advertising, where he leads the vision for next-generation automotive marketing technology, platforms, and strategies focused on outcomes rather than impressions.
- Recognized expert in automotive retail, digital strategy, and integrated media, helping thousands of dealers improve profitability through scalable, ROI-driven campaigns and advanced measurement.
- Proven track record of building high-performing teams and driving digital transformation across the automotive advertising industry.

Innovation and thought leadership

- Architect and early champion of proprietary approaches such as Hypercasting® and Brandcasting, integrating data, creative, and media to reach the right customer with the right message at the right time.
- Key driver behind platforms like Mi4 and MuddVision, which leverage real-time data, predictive modeling, and VIN-level attribution to optimize media performance and eliminate waste.
- Frequent voice on the evolution of automotive marketing, emphasizing outcomes, accountability, and

people-first targeting in partnerships and public commentary.

International speaking and industry presence

Robert Mudd is a sought-after international keynote speaker whose presentations decode complex trends into actionable insights for dealers, motivating teams across continents to rethink traditional marketing and embrace advanced data and technology.

International engagements:

- Keynote Speaker at the inaugural Russia Auto Dealers Association (ROAD) conference in Moscow, Russia (2010), and invited as Workshop Speaker for the

ROAD Delegation at NADA San Francisco (2009)

- Selected Presenter at the inaugural China Automotive Dealers Association (CADA) ATD conference in Chengdu, China (2013)
- Presenter/Participant in the US-China IT Services Exchange Program in Shanghai, China (2013)
- Presenter at European Auto Dealer Day in Verona, Italy (2013)

- Presenter at International Republicans Institute seminars in Bangkok, Thailand (2012) on digital media and web content strategy

North American keynotes and presentations:

- Selected presenter at NADA conventions (2007 Las Vegas, 2014 New Orleans)
- Featured speaker at Digital Dealer Conference & Exposition (Las Vegas, Orlando, Chicago — multiple years)
- Keynote at CPO Vehicles and Balloon Lending, Auto Finance Group, Detroit, MI
- Presenter at Auto Remarketing & CPO Conference (Scottsdale, Phoenix)
- Featured presenter at Pre-Owned Vehicle Department Conferences (Las Vegas, Orlando, Phoenix)
- Speaker at Used Car Week (San Diego, 2014)
- Keynote speaker at CEC Business Technology Conferences (Green Bay, Iowa City)
- Presenter at Family Business Network International Next Generation Conference (New York, NY)

- Speaker at Wards Dealer Business Auto Spring Training Conference (Tampa)
- Speaker at Credit Crisis on Main Street (Washington, D.C.)

ADDITIONAL INDUSTRY CONTRIBUTIONS

- Automotive advertising educator on digital media integration at national conferences
- Featured in podcasts and industry content as "Chief Futurist," sharing perspectives on where automotive media, measurement, and customer engagement are headed next
- Presenter for Comcast Media National Sales Meeting (Salt Lake City)

Career trajectory

- Longstanding leader at Mudd Advertising, progressing from account executive to president roles in digital media and research & development before assuming the Chief Futurist position.
- Built and led high-performing teams in Chicago and Cedar Falls, driving digital innovation, integrated

media strategies, and new business growth for dealership groups nationwide and internationally.

- Early career in B2B sales honed a results-oriented mindset and a focus on building territories and relationships that deliver measurable business impact.

Education and Profile

- Holds a BA in English Literature from the University of Iowa, grounding his analytical and strategic thinking in strong communication and narrative skills.
- Based in Cedar Falls, Iowa, and connected to a broad network of 2,200+ automotive, marketing, and technology professionals across the U.S. and abroad.